UK 2024 Tefal Air XXL Double Drawer Cookbook

2000 Days Easy & Delicious Tefal Easy Fry XXL 2in1 Digital Dual Air Fryer & Grill Recipes for Beginners and Advanced Users

Latrice R. Heflin

All rights reserved worldwide.

No part of this book may be reproduced or transmitted in any form or by any means, electronic or mechanical, including photo copying, recording or by any information storage and retrieval system, without written permission from the publisher, except for the inclusion of brief quotations in a review.

Warning-Disclaimer:

The purpose of this book is to educate and entertain. The author or publisher does not guarantee that anyone following the techniques, suggestions, tips, ideas, or strategies will become successful. The author and publisher shall have neither liability or responsibility to anyone with respect to any loss or damage caused, or alleged to be caused, directly or indirectly by the information contained in this book.

CONTENTS

MEASUREMENT CONVERSIONS 11

Breakfast Recipes 13

Asparagus And Bell Pepper Strata And Greek Bagels 13

Cornbread 13

Blueberry Muffins 14

Honey Banana Oatmeal 14

Bacon And Spinach Egg Muffins 14

Breakfast Cheese Sandwich 15

Wholemeal Banana-walnut Bread 15

Cheddar-ham-corn Muffins 15

Biscuit Balls 16

Double-dipped Mini Cinnamon Biscuits 16

Sesame Bagels 17

Bacon And Egg Omelet 17

Sweet Potato Hash 17

Puff Pastry 18

Easy Pancake Doughnuts 18

Bacon & Spinach Cups 18

Cinnamon Rolls 19

Egg And Avocado In The Tefal 19

Breakfast Potatoes 19

Breakfast Frittata 19

Pork Sausage Eggs With Mustard Sauce 20

Hard Boiled Eggs 20

Egg And Bacon Muffins 21

Bacon Cinnamon Rolls 21

Lemon-blueberry Muffins 21

Salmon Quiche 22

Cinnamon Apple French Toast 22

Savory Sweet Potato Hash 22

Banana And Raisins Muffins 23

Breakfast Pitta 23

Potatoes Lyonnaise 23

Jalapeño Popper Egg Cups And Cheddar Soufflés 24

Air Fried Bacon And Eggs 24

Savory Soufflé 24

Turkey Ham Muffins 25

Cauliflower Avocado Toast And All-in-one Toast 25

Cinnamon Air Fryer Apples 26

Breakfast Sammies 26

Cheesy Baked Eggs 26

Sausage Hash And Baked Eggs 27

Jelly Doughnuts 27

Snacks And Appetizers Recipes 28

Tasty Sweet Potato Wedges 28

Pumpkin Fries 28

JTater Tots 28

alapeño Poppers And Greek Potato Skins With Olives And Feta 29

Stuffed Mushrooms 29

"fried" Ravioli With Zesty Marinara 30

Pretzels 30

Avocado Fries With Sriracha Dip 31

Crispy Tortilla Chips 31

Mozzarella Arancini 31

Stuffed Bell Peppers 32

Crab Cakes 32

Bacon-wrapped Dates Bacon-wrapped Scallops 32

Taco-spiced Chickpeas And Black Bean Corn Dip 33

Miso-glazed Shishito Peppers Charred Lemon Shishito Peppers 33

Mozzarella Sticks 34

Beef Jerky Pineapple Jerky 34

Sausage Balls With Cheese 35

Crispy Plantain Chips 35

Fish And Seafood Recipes 35

Perfect Parmesan Salmon 35

Flavorful Salmon With Green Beans 36

Orange-mustard Glazed Salmon 36

Southwestern Fish Fillets 36

Bacon-wrapped Shrimp 37

Sweet Tilapia Fillets 37

Panko-crusted Fish Sticks 37

Cod With Avocado And Garlic Prawns 38

Tasty Parmesan Shrimp 38

Herb Tuna Patties 39

Herb Lemon Mussels 39

Fish Sandwich 39

Brown Sugar Garlic Salmon 40

Crispy Catfish 40

Salmon Nuggets 40

Bang Bang Shrimp With Roasted Bok Choy 41

Salmon With Broccoli And Cheese 41

Chilean Sea Bass With Olive Relish And Snapper With Tomato 42

Prawn Dejonghe Skewers 42

Tuna Patty Sliders 43

Tilapia With Mojo And Crispy Plantains 43

Pecan-crusted Catfish Nuggets With "fried" Okra 44

Fried Tilapia 44

Seafood Shrimp Omelet 45

Honey Teriyaki Tilapia 45

Butter-wine Baked Salmon 45

Garlic Butter Prawns Scampi & Coconut Prawns 46

Simple Buttery Cod & Salmon On Bed Of Fennel And Carrot 46

Spicy Fish Fillet With Onion Rings 47

Lemon Pepper Fish Fillets 47

Classic Fish Sticks With Tartar Sauce 47

Cajun Catfish Cakes With Cheese 48

Breaded Scallops 48

Honey Pecan Shrimp 48

Codfish With Herb Vinaigrette 49

Blackened Mahimahi With Honey-roasted Carrots 49

Cajun Scallops 50

Thai Prawn Skewers And Lemon-tarragon Fish En Papillote 50

Glazed Scallops 51

Tender Juicy Honey Glazed Salmon 51

Two-way Salmon 51

Poultry Recipes 52

Chicken Thighs With Coriander 52

Turkey Burger Patties 52

Buffalo Chicken 52

Cracked-pepper Chicken Wings 53

Sweet-and-sour Chicken With Pineapple Cauliflower Rice 53

Chipotle Drumsticks 54

Marinated Chicken Legs 54

Chicken Strips With Satay Sauce 54

Garlic Dill Wings 55

Curried Orange Honey Chicken 55

Thai Chicken Meatballs 55

Spice-rubbed Chicken Pieces 56

Simply Terrific Turkey Meatballs 56

Lemon Chicken Thighs 56

Roasted Garlic Chicken Pizza With Cauliflower "wings" 57

Brazilian Chicken Drumsticks 57

Juicy Paprika Chicken Breast 58

Wild Rice And Kale Stuffed Chicken Thighs 58

Buttermilk Fried Chicken 58

General Tso's Chicken 59

Sweet And Spicy Carrots With Chicken Thighs 59

Honey-glazed Chicken Thighs 60

Asian Chicken 60

Teriyaki Chicken Skewers 60

Wings With Corn On The Cob 61

Apricot-glazed Turkey Tenderloin 61

Chicken & Broccoli 61

Fajita Chicken Strips & Barbecued Chicken With Creamy Coleslaw 62

Chicken Shawarma 62

Jamaican Fried Chicken 63

Crumbed Chicken Katsu 63

Chicken Legs With Leeks 64

Yummy Chicken Breasts 64

Chicken Kebabs 64

Orange Chicken With Roasted Snap Peas And Scallions 65

Chicken Vegetable Skewers 65

Goat Cheese–stuffed Chicken Breast With Broiled Zucchini And Cherry Tomatoes 66

Crispy Sesame Chicken 66

Bell Pepper Stuffed Chicken Roll-ups 67

Coconut Chicken Tenders With Broiled Utica Greens 67

Beef, Pork, And Lamb Recipes 68

Bacon Wrapped Pork Tenderloin 68

Easy Breaded Pork Chops	68
Kheema Burgers	68
Strip Steaks With Hasselback Potatoes	69
Air Fryer Meatloaves	69
Spicy Lamb Chops	70
Pork Chops With Broccoli	70
Honey Glazed Bbq Pork Ribs	70
Beef Cheeseburgers	71
Sumptuous Pizza Tortilla Rolls	71
Roasted Beef	71
Bo Luc Lac	72
Mustard Rubbed Lamb Chops	72
Steak Bites With Cowboy Butter	73
Cinnamon-apple Pork Chops	73
Sausage Meatballs	73
Smothered Chops	74
Garlic-rosemary Pork Loin With Scalloped Potatoes And Cauliflower	74
Kielbasa Sausage With Pineapple And Kheema Meatloaf	75
Beef Ribs Ii	75
Bbq Pork Spare Ribs	76
Sausage-stuffed Peppers	76
Cinnamon-beef Kofta	76
Pigs In A Blanket With Spinach-artichoke Stuffed Mushrooms	77
Nigerian Peanut-crusted Bavette Steak	77
Goat Cheese-stuffed Bavette Steak	78
Garlic Sirloin Steak	78
Lamb Shank With Mushroom Sauce	78
Tasty Lamb Patties	79
Sausage And Pork Meatballs	79
Blue Cheese Steak Salad	79
Bacon-wrapped Filet Mignon	80

Italian Sausage And Cheese Meatballs 80

Vegetables And Sides Recipes 80

Mixed Air Fry Veggies 80

Zucchini With Stuffing 81

Green Beans With Baked Potatoes 81

Pepper Poppers 81

Kale And Spinach Chips 82

Fresh Mix Veggies In Air Fryer 82

Brussels Sprouts 82

Fried Asparagus 82

Flavourful Mexican Cauliflower 83

Garlic-herb Fried Squash 83

Beets With Orange Gremolata And Goat's Cheese 83

Potato And Parsnip Latkes With Baked Apples 84

Mushroom Roll-ups 84

Green Salad With Crispy Fried Goat Cheese And Baked Croutons 85

Sweet Potatoes & Brussels Sprouts 85

Buffalo Seitan With Crispy Zucchini Noodles 86

Garlic-rosemary Brussels Sprouts 86

Garlic Herbed Baked Potatoes 87

Jerk Tofu With Roasted Cabbage 87

Desserts Recipes 88

Crustless Peanut Butter Cheesecake And Pumpkin Pudding With Vanilla Wafers 88

Apple Nutmeg Flautas 88

Apple Fritters 89

Delicious Apple Fritters 89

Fried Oreos 89

Banana Spring Rolls With Hot Fudge Dip 90

Simple Pineapple Sticks And Crispy Pineapple Rings 90

Easy Mini Chocolate Chip Pan Cookie 91

Coconut-custard Pie And Pecan Brownies 91

Air Fried Bananas 91

Chocolate Mug Cakes 92

Mini Peanut Butter Tarts 92

Air Fried Beignets 93

S'mores Dip With Cinnamon-sugar Tortillas 93

Pumpkin-spice Bread Pudding 94

Maple-pecan Tart With Sea Salt 94

Simple Cheesecake 95

Pumpkin Hand Pies Blueberry Hand Pies 95

Bread Pudding 96

Gluten-free Spice Cookies 96

Pecan Brownies And Cinnamon-sugar Almonds 96

Cinnamon Sugar Dessert Fries 97

Berry Crumble And S'mores 97

Cream Cheese Shortbread Cookies 97

Peanut Butter, Honey & Banana Toast 98

Grilled Peaches 98

Walnut Baklava Bites Pistachio Baklava Bites 98

Cinnamon Bread Twists 99

Funnel Cake 99

Healthy Semolina Pudding 99

Pumpkin Muffins 100

RECIPES INDEX 101

MEASUREMENT CONVERSIONS

BASIC KITCHEN CONVERSIONS & EQUIVALENTS

DRY MEASUREMENTS CONVERSION CHART

3 TEASPOONS = 1 TABLESPOON = 1/16 CUP
6 TEASPOONS = 2 TABLESPOONS = 1/8 CUP
12 TEASPOONS = 4 TABLESPOONS = 1/4 CUP
24 TEASPOONS = 8 TABLESPOONS = 1/2 CUP
36 TEASPOONS = 12 TABLESPOONS = 3/4 CUP
48 TEASPOONS = 16 TABLESPOONS = 1 CUP

METRIC TO US COOKING CONVER-SIONS

OVEN TEMPERATURES

120 °C = 250 °F
160 °C = 320 °F
180 °C = 350 °F
205 °C = 400 °F
220 °C = 425 °F

LIQUID MEASUREMENTS CONVERSION CHART

8 FLUID OUNCES = 1 CUP = 1/2 PINT = 1/4 QUART
16 FLUID OUNCES = 2 CUPS = 1 PINT = 1/2 QUART
32 FLUID OUNCES = 4 CUPS = 2 PINTS = 1 QUART
1/4 GALLON
128 FLUID OUNCES = 16 CUPS = 8 PINTS = 4 QUARTS = 1 GALLON

BAKING IN GRAMS

1 CUP FLOUR = 140 GRAMS
1 CUP SUGAR = 150 GRAMS
1 CUP POWDERED SUGAR=160 GRAMS
1 CUP HEAVY CREAM = 235 GRAMS

VOLUME

1 MILLILITER=1/5 TEASPOON
5 ML = 1 TEASPOON
15 ML = 1 TABLESPOON
240 ML = 1 CUP OR 8 FLUID OUNCES
1 LITER=34 FL. OUNCES

WEIGHT

1 GRAM = 035 OUNCES
100 GRAMS=3.5 OUNCES
500 GRAMS = 1.1 POUNDS
1 KILOGRAM=35 OUNCES

US TO METRIC COOKING CONVERSIONS

1/5 TSP = 1 ML
1 TSP=5 ML
1 TBSP = 15 ML
1 FL OUNCE = 30 ML
1 CUP=237 ML
1 PINT (2 CUPS) = 473 ML
1 QUART (4 CUPS)=.95 LITER
1GALLON (16 CUPS)=3.8LITERS
1 0Z=28 GRAMS
1 POUND = 454 GRAMS

BUTTER

1 CUP BUTTER=2 STICKS = 8 OUNCES = 230 GRAMS=8 TABLESPOONS

WHAT DOES 1 CUP EQUAL

1 CUP = 8 FLUID OUNCES
1 CUP = 16 TABLESPOONS
1 CUP = 48 TEASPOONS
1 CUP = 1/2 PINT
1 CUP = 1/4 QUART
1 CUP = 1/16 GALLON
1 CUP = 240 ML

BAKING PAN CONVERSIONS

1 CUP ALL-PURPOSE FLOUR=4.5 OZ
1 CUP ROLLED OATS = 3 OZ 1 LARGE EGG = 1.7 OZ
1 CUP BUTTER=8OZ 1 CUP MILK = 8 OZ
1 CUP HEAVY CREAM = 8.4 OZ
1 CUP GRANULATED SUGAR=7.1 OZ
1 CUP PACKED BROWN SUGAR = 7.75 OZ
1 CUP VEGETABLE OIL = 7.7 OZ
1 CUP UNSIFTED POWDERED SUGAR = 4.4 OZ

BAKING PAN CONVERSIONS

9-INCH ROUND CAKE PAN= 12 CUPS
10-INCH TUBE PAN =16 CUPS
11-INCH BUNDT PAN = 12 CUPS
9-INCH SPRINGFORM PAN = 10 CUPS
9 X 5 INCH LOAF PAN=8 CUPS
9-INCH SQUARE PAN=8 CUPS

Breakfast Recipes

Asparagus And Bell Pepper Strata And Greek Bagels

Servings: 6
Cooking Time: 14 To 20 Minutes
Ingredients:
- Asparagus and Bell Pepper Strata:
- 8 large asparagus spears, trimmed and cut into 2-inch pieces
- 80 ml shredded carrot
- 120 ml chopped red pepper
- 2 slices wholemeal bread, cut into ½-inch cubes
- 3 egg whites
- 1 egg
- 3 tablespoons 1% milk
- ½ teaspoon dried thyme
- Greek Bagels:
- 120 ml self-raising flour, plus more for dusting
- 120 ml plain Greek yoghurt
- 1 egg
- 1 tablespoon water
- 4 teaspoons sesame seeds or za'atar
- Cooking oil spray
- 1 tablespoon butter, melted

Directions:
1. Make the Asparagus and Bell Pepper Strata :
2. In a baking pan, combine the asparagus, carrot, red bell pepper, and 1 tablespoon of water. Bake in the air fryer at 166°C for 3 to 5 minutes, or until crisp-tender. Drain well.
3. Add the bread cubes to the vegetables and gently toss.
4. In a medium bowl, whisk the egg whites, egg, milk, and thyme until frothy.
5. Pour the egg mixture into the pan. Bake in the zone 1 drawer for 11 to 15 minutes, or until the strata is slightly puffy and set and the top starts to brown. Serve.
6. Make the Greek Bagels :
7. In a large bowl, using a wooden spoon, stir together the flour and yoghurt until a tacky dough forms. Transfer the dough to a lightly floured work surface and roll the dough into a ball.
8. Cut the dough into 2 pieces and roll each piece into a log. Form each log into a bagel shape, pinching the ends together.
9. In a small bowl, whisk the egg and water. Brush the egg wash on the bagels.
10. Sprinkle 2 teaspoons of the toppings on each bagel and gently press it into the dough.
11. Insert the crisper plate into the zone 2 drawer and the drawer into the unit. Preheat the drawer by selecting BAKE, setting the temperature to 166°C, and setting the time to 3 minutes. Select START/STOP to begin.
12. Once the drawer is preheated, spray the crisper plate with cooking spray. Drizzle the bagels with the butter and place them into the drawer.
13. Select BAKE, set the temperature to 166°C, and set the time to 10 minutes. Select START/STOP to begin.
14. When the cooking is complete, the bagels should be lightly golden on the outside. Serve warm.

Cornbread

Servings: 6
Cooking Time: 15 Minutes
Ingredients:
- 1 cup cornmeal
- 1 cup all-purpose flour
- 1 tablespoon sugar
- 2 teaspoons baking powder
- ½ teaspoon baking soda
- ½ teaspoon salt
- 1 stick butter melted
- 1½ cups buttermilk
- 2 eggs
- 113g diced chiles

Directions:
1. Mix cornmeal with flour, sugar, baking powder, baking soda, salt, butter, milk, eggs and chiles in a bowl until smooth.
2. Spread this mixture in two greased 4-inch baking pans.
3. Place one pan in each air fryer basket.
4. Return the air fryer basket 1 to Zone 1, and basket 2 to Zone 2 of the Tefal 2-Basket Air Fryer.
5. Choose the "Air Fry" mode for Zone 1 at 330 degrees F and 15 minutes of cooking time.
6. Select the "MATCH COOK" option to copy the settings for Zone 2.
7. Initiate cooking by pressing the START/PAUSE BUTTON.
8. Slice and serve.

Nutrition:
- (Per serving) Calories 199 | Fat 11.1g | Sodium 297mg | Carbs 14.9g | Fiber 1g | Sugar 2.5g | Protein 9.9g

Blueberry Muffins

Servings: 12
Cooking Time: 12 Minutes
Ingredients:
- 2 egg, beaten
- 2 ripe bananas, peeled and mashed
- 220g almond flour
- 4 tablespoons granulated sugar
- 1 teaspoon baking powder
- 2 tablespoons coconut oil, melted
- 80g maple syrup
- 2 teaspoons apple cider vinegar
- 2 teaspoons vanilla extract
- 2 teaspoons lemon zest, grated
- Pinch of ground cinnamon
- 150g fresh blueberries

Directions:
1. In a large bowl, add all the ingredients except blueberries and mix until well combined.
2. Gently fold in the blueberries.
3. Grease 2 muffin tins.
4. Place the mixture into prepared muffin cups about ¾ full.
5. Press your chosen zone - "Zone 1" or "Zone 2" and then rotate the knob to select "Bake".
6. Set the temperature to 190 degrees C and then set the time for 5 minutes to preheat.
7. After preheating, arrange 1 muffin tin into the basket of each zone.
8. Slide the basket into the Air Fryer and set the time for 12 minutes.
9. After cooking time is completed, remove the muffin tins from Air Fryer.
10. Place both tins onto a wire rack to cool for 10 minutes.
11. Invert the blueberry muffins onto the wire rack to cool completely before serving.

Honey Banana Oatmeal

Servings: 4
Cooking Time: 8 Minutes
Ingredients:
- 2 eggs
- 2 tbsp honey
- 1 tsp vanilla
- 45g quick oats
- 73ml milk
- 30g Greek yoghurt
- 219g banana, mashed

Directions:
1. In a bowl, mix eggs, milk, yoghurt, honey, vanilla, oats, and mashed banana until well combined.
2. Pour batter into the four greased ramekins.
3. Insert a crisper plate in the Tefal air fryer baskets.
4. Place ramekins in both baskets.
5. Select zone 1 then select "air fry" mode and set the temperature to 390 degrees F for 8 minutes. Press "match" to match zone 2 settings to zone 1. Press "start/stop" to begin.

Nutrition:
- (Per serving) Calories 228 | Fat 4.6g | Sodium 42mg | Carbs 40.4g | Fiber 4.2g | Sugar 16.1g | Protein 7.7g

Bacon And Spinach Egg Muffins

Servings: 6
Cooking Time: 12 To 14 Minutes
Ingredients:
- 6 large eggs
- 60 ml double (whipping) cream
- ½ teaspoon sea salt
- ¼ teaspoon freshly ground black pepper
- ¼ teaspoon cayenne pepper (optional)
- 180 ml frozen chopped spinach, thawed and drained
- 4 strips cooked bacon, crumbled
- 60 g shredded Cheddar cheese

Directions:
1. In a large bowl, whisk together the eggs, double cream, salt, black pepper, and cayenne pepper.
2. Divide the spinach and bacon among 6 silicone muffin cups. Place the muffin cups in the zone 1 air fryer drawer.
3. Divide the egg mixture among the muffin cups. Top with the cheese.
4. Set the temperature to 150°C. Bake for 12 to 14 minutes, until the eggs are set and cooked through.

Breakfast Cheese Sandwich

Servings: 2
Cooking Time: 8 Minutes
Ingredients:
- 4 bread slices
- 2 provolone cheese slice
- ¼ tsp dried basil
- 2 tbsp mayonnaise
- 2 Monterey jack cheese slice
- 2 cheddar cheese slice
- ¼ tsp dried oregano

Directions:
1. In a small bowl, mix mayonnaise, basil, and oregano.
2. Spread mayonnaise on one side of the two bread slices.
3. Top two bread slices with cheddar cheese, provolone cheese, Monterey jack cheese slice, and cover with remaining bread slices.
4. Insert a crisper plate in the Tefal air fryer baskets.
5. Place sandwiches in both baskets.
6. Select zone 1, then select "air fry" mode and set the temperature to 390 degrees F for 8 minutes. Press "match" to match zone 2 settings to zone 1. Press "start/stop" to begin. Turn halfway through.

Nutrition:
- (Per serving) Calories 421 | Fat 30.7g |Sodium 796mg | Carbs 13.9g | Fiber 0.5g | Sugar 2.2g | Protein 22.5g

Wholemeal Banana-walnut Bread

Servings: 6
Cooking Time: 23 Minutes
Ingredients:
- Olive oil cooking spray
- 2 ripe medium bananas
- 1 large egg
- 60 ml non-fat plain Greek yoghurt
- 60 ml olive oil
- ½ teaspoon vanilla extract
- 2 tablespoons honey
- 235 ml wholemeal flour
- ¼ teaspoon salt
- ¼ teaspoon baking soda
- ½ teaspoon ground cinnamon
- 60 ml chopped walnuts

Directions:
1. Lightly coat the inside of two 5 ½-by-3-inch loaf pans with olive oil cooking spray.
2. In a large bowl, mash the bananas with a fork. Add the egg, yoghurt, olive oil, vanilla, and honey. Mix until well combined and mostly smooth. Sift the wholemeal flour, salt, baking soda, and cinnamon into the wet mixture, then stir until just combined. Do not overmix. Gently fold in the walnuts. Pour into the prepared loaf pans and spread to distribute evenly.
3. Place a loaf pan in the zone 1 drawer and another pan into zone 2 drawer. In zone 1, select Bake button and adjust temperature to 180°C, set time to 20 to 23 minutes. In zone 2, select Match Cook and press Start.
4. Remove until golden brown on top and a toothpick inserted into the center comes out clean. Allow to cool for 5 minutes before serving.

Cheddar-ham-corn Muffins

Servings: 8 Muffins
Cooking Time: 6 To 8 Minutes
Ingredients:
- 180 ml cornmeal/polenta
- 60 ml flour
- 1½ teaspoons baking powder
- ¼ teaspoon salt
- 1 egg, beaten
- 2 tablespoons rapeseed oil
- 120 ml milk
- 120 ml shredded sharp Cheddar cheese
- 120 ml diced ham
- 8 foil muffin cups, liners removed and sprayed with cooking spray

Directions:
1. Preheat the air fryer to 200°C.
2. In a medium bowl, stir together the cornmeal, flour, baking powder, and salt.
3. Add egg, oil, and milk to dry ingredients and mix well.
4. Stir in shredded cheese and diced ham.
5. Divide batter among the muffin cups.
6. Place filled muffin cups in two air fryer drawers and bake for 5 minutes.
7. Reduce temperature to 166°C and bake for 1 to 2 minutes or until toothpick inserted in center of muffin comes out clean.

Biscuit Balls

Servings: 6
Cooking Time: 18 Minutes.

Ingredients:
- 1 tablespoon butter
- 2 eggs, beaten
- ¼ teaspoon pepper
- 1 can (10.2-oz) Pillsbury Buttermilk biscuits
- 2 ounces cheddar cheese, diced into ten cubes
- Cooking spray
- Egg Wash
- 1 egg
- 1 tablespoon water

Directions:
1. Place a suitable non-stick skillet over medium-high heat and cook the bacon until crispy, then place it on a plate lined with a paper towel.
2. Melt butter in the same skillet over medium heat. Beat eggs with pepper in a bowl and pour them into the skillet.
3. Stir cook for 5 minutes, then remove it from the heat.
4. Add bacon and mix well.
5. Divide the dough into 5 biscuits and slice each into 2 layers.
6. Press each biscuit into 4-inch round.
7. Add a tablespoon of the egg mixture at the center of each round and top it with a piece of cheese.
8. Carefully fold the biscuit dough around the filling and pinch the edges to seal.
9. Whisk egg with water in a small bowl and brush the egg wash over the biscuits.
10. Place half of the biscuit bombs in each of the crisper plate and spray them with cooking oil.
11. Return the crisper plate to the Tefal Dual Zone Air Fryer.
12. Choose the Air Fry mode for Zone 1 and set the temperature to 375 degrees F and the time to 14 minutes.
13. Select the "MATCH" button to copy the settings for Zone 2.
14. Initiate cooking by pressing the START/STOP button.
15. Flip the egg bombs when cooked halfway through, then resume cooking.
16. Serve warm.

Nutrition:
- (Per serving) Calories 102 | Fat 7.6g | Sodium 545mg | Carbs 1.5g | Fiber 0.4g | Sugar 0.7g | Protein 7.1g

Double-dipped Mini Cinnamon Biscuits

Servings: 8 Biscuits
Cooking Time: 13 Minutes

Ingredients:
- 475 ml blanched almond flour
- 120 ml liquid or powdered sweetener
- 1 teaspoon baking powder
- ½ teaspoon fine sea salt
- 60 ml plus 2 tablespoons (¾ stick) very cold unsalted butter
- 60 ml unsweetened, unflavoured almond milk
- 1 large egg
- 1 teaspoon vanilla extract
- 3 teaspoons ground cinnamon
- Glaze:
- 120 ml powdered sweetener
- 60 ml double cream or unsweetened, unflavoured almond milk

Directions:
1. Preheat the air fryer to 175°C. Line a pie pan that fits into your air fryer with parchment paper. 2. In a medium-sized bowl, mix together the almond flour, sweetener, baking powder, and salt. Cut the butter into ½-inch squares, then use a hand mixer to work the butter into the dry ingredients. When you are done, the mixture should still have chunks of butter. 3. In a small bowl, whisk together the almond milk, egg, and vanilla extract until blended. Using a fork, stir the wet ingredients into the dry ingredients until large clumps form. Add the cinnamon and use your hands to swirl it into the dough. 4. Form the dough into sixteen 1-inch balls and place them on the prepared pan, spacing them about ½ inch apart. Bake in the zone 1 air fryer basket until golden, 10 to 13 minutes. Remove from the air fryer and let cool on the pan for at least 5 minutes. 5. While the biscuits bake, make the glaze: Place the powdered sweetener in a small bowl and slowly stir in the heavy cream with a fork. 6. When the biscuits have cooled somewhat, dip the tops into the glaze, allow it to dry a bit, and then dip again for a thick glaze. 7. Serve warm or at room temperature. Store unglazed biscuits in an airtight container in the refrigerator for up to 3 days or in the freezer for up to a month. Reheat in a preheated 175°C air fryer for 5 minutes, or until warmed through, and dip in the glaze as instructed above.

Sesame Bagels

Servings: 4
Cooking Time: 15 Minutes
Ingredients:
- 125g self-rising flour
- 240g non-fat plain Greek yoghurt
- 1 beaten egg
- 30g sesame seeds

Directions:
1. Combine the self-rising flour and Greek yoghurt in a medium mixing bowl using a wooden spoon.
2. Knead the dough for about 5 minutes on a lightly floured board.
3. Divide the dough into four equal pieces and roll each into a thin rope, securing the ends to form a bagel shape. Sprinkle the sesame seeds on it.
4. Press either "Zone 1" or "Zone 2" and then rotate the knob to select "Air Fryer".
5. Set the temperature to 140 degrees C, and then set the time for 3 minutes to preheat.
6. After preheating, arrange bagels into the basket.
7. Slide basket into Air Fryer and set the time for 15 minutes.
8. After cooking time is completed, remove both pans from Air Fryer.
9. Place the bagels onto a wire rack to cool for about 10 minutes and serve.

Bacon And Egg Omelet

Servings:2
Cooking Time:10
Ingredients:
- 2 eggs, whisked
- ½ teaspoon of chopped tomatoes
- Sea Salt and black pepper, to taste
- 2 teaspoons of almond milk
- 1 teaspoon of cilantro, chopped
- 1 small green chili, chopped
- 4 slices of bacon

Directions:
1. Take a bowl and whisk eggs in it.
2. Then add green chili salt, black pepper, cilantro, almond milk, and chopped tomatoes.
3. Oil greases the ramekins.
4. Pour this into ramekins.
5. Put the bacon in the zone 1 basket and ramekins in zone 2 basket of the Tefal 2-Basket Air Fryer.
6. Now for zone 1, set it to AIR FRY mode at 400 degrees F for 10 minutes
7. And for zone 2, set it 350 degrees for 10 minutes in AIR FRY mode.
8. Press the Smart finish button and press start, it will finish both at the same time.
9. Once done, serve and enjoy.

Nutrition:
- (Per serving) Calories 285| Fat 21.5g| Sodium1000 mg | Carbs 2.2g | Fiber 0.1g| Sugar1 g | Protein 19.7g

Sweet Potato Hash

Servings: 4
Cooking Time: 15 Minutes
Ingredients:
- 3 sweet potatoes, peel & cut into ½-inch pieces
- ½ tsp cinnamon
- 2 tbsp olive oil
- 1 bell pepper, cut into ½-inch pieces
- ½ tsp dried thyme
- ½ tsp nutmeg
- 1 medium onion, cut into ½-inch pieces
- Pepper
- Salt

Directions:
1. In a bowl, toss sweet potatoes with the remaining ingredients.
2. Insert a crisper plate in Tefal air fryer baskets.
3. Add potato mixture in both baskets.
4. Select zone 1 then select "air fry" mode and set the temperature to 355 degrees F for 15 minutes. Press "match" to match zone 2 settings to zone 1. Press "start/stop" to begin.

Nutrition:
- (Per serving) Calories 167 | Fat 7.3g |Sodium 94mg | Carbs 24.9g | Fiber 4.2g | Sugar 6.8g | Protein 2.2g

Puff Pastry

Servings: 6
Cooking Time: 10 Minutes
Ingredients:
- 1 package (200g) cream cheese, softened
- 50g sugar
- 2 tablespoons plain flour
- ½ teaspoon vanilla extract
- 2 large egg yolks
- 1 tablespoon water
- 1 package frozen puff pastry, thawed
- 210g seedless raspberry jam

Directions:
1. Mix the cream cheese, sugar, flour, and vanilla extract until smooth, then add 1 egg yolk.
2. Combine the remaining egg yolk with the water. Unfold each sheet of puff pastry on a lightly floured board and roll into a 30 cm square. Cut into nine 10 cm squares.
3. Put 1 tablespoon cream cheese mixture and 1 rounded teaspoon jam on each. Bring 2 opposite corners of pastry over filling, sealing with yolk mixture.
4. Brush the remaining yolk mixture over the tops.
5. Press your chosen zone - "Zone 1" or "Zone 2" and then rotate the knob to select "Air Fry".
6. Set the temperature to 160 degrees C, and then set the time for 5 minutes to preheat.
7. After preheating, spray the Air-Fryer basket of each zone with cooking spray, line them with parchment paper, and place the pastry on them.
8. Slide the basket into the Air Fryer and set the time for 10 minutes.
9. After cooking time is completed, transfer them onto serving plates and serve.

Easy Pancake Doughnuts

Servings: 8
Cooking Time: 9 Minutes
Ingredients:
- 2 eggs
- 50g sugar
- 125ml vegetable oil
- 240g pancake mix
- 1 ½ tbsp cinnamon

Directions:
1. In a bowl, mix pancake mix, eggs, cinnamon, sugar, and oil until well combined.
2. Pour the doughnut mixture into the silicone doughnut moulds.
3. Insert a crisper plate in Tefal air fryer baskets.
4. Place doughnut moulds in both baskets.
5. Select zone 1 then select "air fry" mode and set the temperature to 355 degrees F for 9 minutes. Press "match" to match zone 2 settings to zone 1. Press "start/stop" to begin.

Nutrition:
- (Per serving) Calories 163 | Fat 14.7g |Sodium 16mg | Carbs 7.4g | Fiber 0.7g | Sugar 6.4g | Protein 1.4g

Bacon & Spinach Cups

Servings: 6
Cooking Time: 19 Minutes
Ingredients:
- 6 eggs
- 12 bacon slices, chopped
- 120g fresh baby spinach
- 180g heavy cream
- 6 tablespoons Parmesan cheese, grated
- Salt and ground black pepper, as required

Directions:
1. Heat a non-stick frying pan over medium-high heat and cook the bacon for about 6-8 minutes.
2. Add the spinach and cook for about 2-3 minutes.
3. Stir in the heavy cream and Parmesan cheese and cook for about 2-3 minutes.
4. Remove from the heat and set aside to cool slightly.
5. Press "Zone 1" and "Zone 2" of Tefal 2-Basket Air Fryer and then rotate the knob for each zone to select "Air Fry".
6. Set the temperature to 175 degrees C and then set the time for 5 minutes to preheat.
7. Crack 1 egg in each of 6 greased ramekins and top with bacon mixture.
8. After preheating, arrange 3 ramekins into the basket of each zone.
9. Slide the basket into the Air Fryer and set the time for 5 minutes.
10. After cooking time is completed, remove the ramekins from Air Fryer.
11. Sprinkle the top of each cup with salt and black pepper and serve hot.

Cinnamon Rolls

Servings: 12 Rolls
Cooking Time: 20 Minutes
Ingredients:
- 600 ml shredded Mozzarella cheese
- 60 g cream cheese, softened
- 235 ml blanched finely ground almond flour
- ½ teaspoon vanilla extract
- 120 ml icing sugar-style sweetener
- 1 tablespoon ground cinnamon

Directions:
1. In a large microwave-safe bowl, combine Mozzarella cheese, cream cheese, and flour. Microwave the mixture on high 90 seconds until cheese is melted.
2. Add vanilla extract and sweetener, and mix 2 minutes until a dough forms.
3. Once the dough is cool enough to work with your hands, about 2 minutes, spread it out into a 12 × 4-inch rectangle on ungreased parchment paper. Evenly sprinkle dough with cinnamon.
4. Starting at the long side of the dough, roll lengthwise to form a log. Slice the log into twelve even pieces.
5. Divide rolls between two ungreased round nonstick baking dishes. Place the dishes into the two air fryer drawers. Adjust the temperature to 192°C and bake for 10 minutes.
6. Cinnamon rolls will be done when golden around the edges and mostly firm. Allow rolls to cool in dishes 10 minutes before serving.

Egg And Avocado In The Tefal

Servings: 2
Cooking Time: 12
Ingredients:
- 2 Avocados, pitted and cut in half
- Garlic salt, to taste
- Cooking for greasing
- 4 eggs
- ¼ teaspoon of Paprika powder, for sprinkling
- 1/3 cup parmesan cheese, crumbled
- 6 bacon strips, raw

Directions:
1. First cut the avocado in half and pit it.
2. Now scoop out the flesh from the avocado and keep intact some of it
3. Crack one egg in each hole of avocado and sprinkle paprika and garlic salt
4. Top it with cheese at the end.
5. Now put it into tin foils and then put it in the air fryer zone basket 1
6. Put bacon strips in zone 2 basket.
7. Now for zone 1, set it to AIR FRY mode at 350 degrees F for 10 minutes
8. And for zone 2, set it 400 degrees for 12 minutes AIR FRY mode.
9. Press the Smart finish button and press start, it will finish both at the same time.
10. Once done, serve and enjoy.

Nutrition:
- (Per serving) Calories609 | Fat53.2g | Sodium 335mg | Carbs 18.1g | Fiber13.5g | Sugar 1.7g | Protein 21.3g

Breakfast Potatoes

Servings: 6
Cooking Time: 20 Minutes
Ingredients:
- 3 russet potatoes, cut into bite-sized pieces with skin on
- 1 teaspoon garlic powder
- 1 teaspoon onion powder
- 2 teaspoons fine ground sea salt
- 1 teaspoon black pepper
- 1 tablespoon olive oil
- ½ red pepper, diced

Directions:
1. The potatoes should be washed and scrubbed before being sliced into bite-sized pieces with the skin on.
2. Using paper towels, dry them and place them in a large mixing bowl.
3. Toss in the spices and drizzle with olive oil. Stir in the pepper until everything is completely combined.
4. Line a basket with parchment paper.
5. Press either "Zone 1" or "Zone 2" and then rotate the knob to select "Air Fryer".
6. Set the temperature to 195 degrees C, and then set the time for 3 minutes to preheat.
7. After preheating, spread the potatoes in a single layer on the sheet.
8. Slide basket into Air Fryer and set the time for 15 minutes.
9. After cooking time is completed, remove basket from Air Fryer.
10. Place them on serving plates and serve.

Breakfast Frittata

Servings: 4

Cooking Time: 12 Minutes
Ingredients:
- 4 eggs
- 4 tablespoons milk
- 35g cheddar cheese grated
- 50g feta crumbled
- 1 tomato, deseeded and chopped
- 15g spinach chopped
- 1 tablespoon fresh herbs, chopped
- 2 spring onion chopped
- Salt and black pepper, to taste
- ½ teaspoon olive oil

Directions:
1. Beat eggs with milk in a bowl and stir in the rest of the ingredients.
2. Grease two small-sized springform pans and line them with parchment paper.
3. Divide the egg mixture into the pans and place one in each air fryer basket.
4. Return the air fryer basket 1 to Zone 1, and basket 2 to Zone 2 of the Tefal 2-Basket Air Fryer.
5. Choose the "Air Fry" mode for Zone 1 at 350 degrees F and 12 minutes of cooking time.
6. Select the "MATCH COOK" option to copy the settings for Zone 2.
7. Initiate cooking by pressing the START/PAUSE BUTTON.
8. Serve warm.

Nutrition:
- (Per serving) Calories 273 | Fat 22g |Sodium 517mg | Carbs 3.3g | Fiber 0.2g | Sugar 1.4g | Protein 16.1g

Pork Sausage Eggs With Mustard Sauce

Servings: 8
Cooking Time: 12 Minutes
Ingredients:
- 450 g pork sausage meat
- 8 soft-boiled or hard-boiled eggs, peeled
- 1 large egg
- 2 tablespoons milk
- 235 ml crushed pork scratchings
- Smoky Mustard Sauce:
- 60 ml mayonnaise
- 2 tablespoons sour cream
- 1 tablespoon Dijon mustard
- 1 teaspoon chipotle hot sauce

Directions:
1. Divide the sausage into 8 portions. Take each portion of sausage, pat it down into a patty, and place 1 egg in the middle, gently wrapping the sausage around the egg until the egg is completely covered.
2. Repeat with the remaining eggs and sausage. In a small shallow bowl, whisk the egg and milk until frothy. In another shallow bowl, place the crushed pork scratchings. Working one at a time, dip a sausage-wrapped egg into the beaten egg and then into the pork scratchings, gently rolling to coat evenly. Repeat with the remaining sausage-wrapped eggs.
3. Put them half in zone 1, the remaining in zone 2. Lightly spray with olive oil. In zone 1 , select Air fry button, adjust temperature to 200°C, set time to 10 to 12 minutes. In zone 2, select Match Cook and press Start. Pause halfway through the baking time to turn the eggs, until the eggs are hot and the sausage is cooked through.
4. To make the sauce:
5. In a small bowl, combine the mayonnaise, sour cream, Dijon, and hot sauce. Whisk until thoroughly combined. Serve with the Scotch eggs.

Hard Boiled Eggs

Servings: 6
Cooking Time: 18 Minutes
Ingredients:
- 6 eggs
- Cold water

Directions:
1. Press your chosen zone - "Zone 1" or "Zone 2" and then rotate the knob to select "Air Fryer".
2. Set the temperature to 120 degrees C, and then set the time for 5 minutes to preheat.
3. After preheating, arrange eggs into the basket of each zone.
4. Slide the baskets into Air Fryer and set the time for 18 minutes.
5. After cooking time is completed, transfer the eggs into cold water and serve.

Egg And Bacon Muffins

Servings: 1
Cooking Time: 15 Minutes
Ingredients:
- 2 eggs
- Salt and ground black pepper, to taste
- 1 tablespoon green pesto
- 85 g shredded Cheddar cheese
- 140 g cooked bacon
- 1 spring onion, chopped

Directions:
1. Line a cupcake tin with parchment paper. Beat the eggs with pepper, salt, and pesto in a bowl. Mix in the cheese.
2. Pour the eggs into the cupcake tin and top with the bacon and spring onion.
3. Place the cupcake tin into the zone 1 drawer and bake at 180°C for 15 minutes, or until the egg is set. Serve immediately.

Bacon Cinnamon Rolls

Servings: 8
Cooking Time: 10 Minutes
Ingredients:
- 8 bacon strips
- 180ml bourbon
- 1 tube (310g) refrigerated cinnamon rolls with icing
- 55g chopped pecans
- 2 tablespoons maple syrup

Directions:
1. In a small bowl, combine the bacon and the bourbon. Refrigerate overnight after sealing. Remove the bacon and pat it dry; toss out the bourbon.
2. Cook bacon in batches in a large frying pan over medium heat until nearly crisp but still flexible. Remove to a plate lined with paper towels to drain.
3. Separate the dough into 8 rolls and set aside the frosting packet. Spiral rolls should be unrolled into long strips.
4. Place 1 bacon strip on each dough strip, cut as necessary, and reroll to form a spiral. To seal the ends, pinch them together.
5. Press your chosen zone - "Zone 1" or "Zone 2" and then rotate the knob to select "Air Fry".
6. Set the temperature to 175 degrees C, and then set the time for 5 minutes to preheat.
7. After preheating, spray the Air-Fryer basket of each zone with cooking spray, line them with parchment paper, and place rolls.
8. Slide the basket into the Air Fryer and set the time for 5 minutes.
9. Turn the rolls over and cook for another 4 minutes, or until golden brown.
10. Meanwhile, combine the pecans and maple syrup in a mixing bowl. In a separate bowl, combine the contents of the icing packet.
11. Heat the remaining bacon drippings in the same frying pan over medium heat. Cook, stirring regularly until the pecan mixture is gently browned, about 2-3 minutes.
12. After cooking time is completed, transfer them onto serving plates and drizzle half the icing over warm cinnamon rolls; top with half the pecans.

Lemon-blueberry Muffins

Servings: 6 Muffins
Cooking Time: 20 To 25 Minutes
Ingredients:
- 300 ml almond flour
- 3 tablespoons granulated sweetener
- 1 teaspoon baking powder
- 2 large eggs
- 3 tablespoons melted butter
- 1 tablespoon almond milk
- 1 tablespoon fresh lemon juice
- 120 ml fresh blueberries

Directions:
1. Preheat the zone 1 air fryer drawer to 176°C. Lightly coat 6 silicone muffin cups with vegetable oil. Set aside.
2. In a large mixing bowl, combine the almond flour, sweetener, and baking soda. Set aside.
3. In a separate small bowl, whisk together the eggs, butter, milk, and lemon juice. Add the egg mixture to the flour mixture and stir until just combined. Fold in the blueberries and let the batter sit for 5 minutes.
4. Spoon the muffin batter into the muffin cups, about two-thirds full. Air fry in the zone 1 drawer for 20 to 25 minutes, or until a toothpick inserted into the center of a muffin comes out clean.
5. Remove the drawer from the air fryer and let the muffins cool for about 5 minutes before transferring them to a wire rack to cool completely.

Salmon Quiche

Servings: 4
Cooking Time: 20 Minutes
Ingredients:
- 275g salmon fillets, chopped
- Salt and ground black pepper, as required
- 1 tablespoon fresh lemon juice
- 2 egg yolks
- 7 tablespoons chilled butter
- 165g flour
- 2 tablespoons cold water
- 4 eggs
- 6 tablespoons whipping cream
- 2 spring onions, chopped

Directions:
1. In a bowl, mix together the salmon, salt, black pepper and lemon juice. Set aside.
2. In another bowl, add egg yolk, butter, flour and water and mix until a dough forms.
3. Divide the dough into 2 portions.
4. Place each dough onto a floured smooth surface and roll into about 17.5cm round.
5. Place each rolled dough into a quiche pan and press firmly in the bottom and along the edges.
6. Then trim the excess edges.
7. In a small bowl, add the eggs, cream, salt and black pepper and beat until well combined.
8. Place the cream mixture over each crust evenly and top with the salmon, followed by the spring onion.
9. Press either "Zone 1" or "Zone 2" of Tefal 2-Basket Air Fryer and then rotate the knob for each zone to select "Air Fry".
10. Set the temperature to 180 degrees C and then set the time for 5 minutes to preheat.
11. After preheating, arrange 1 quiche pan into the basket of each zone.
12. Slide the basket into the Air Fryer and set the time for 20 minutes.
13. After cooking time is completed, remove the quiche pans from Air Fryer.
14. Cut each quiche in 2 portions and serve hot.

Cinnamon Apple French Toast

Servings: 8
Cooking Time: 10 Minutes
Ingredients:
- 1 egg, lightly beaten
- 4 bread slices
- 1 tbsp cinnamon
- 15ml milk
- 23ml maple syrup
- 45 ml applesauce

Directions:
1. In a bowl, whisk egg, milk, cinnamon, applesauce, and maple syrup.
2. Insert a crisper plate in the Tefal air fryer baskets.
3. Dip each slice in egg mixture and place in both baskets.
4. Select zone 1 then select "air fry" mode and set the temperature to 355 degrees F for 10 minutes. Press "match" to match zone 2 settings to zone 1. Press "start/stop" to begin.

Nutrition:
- (Per serving) Calories 64 | Fat 1.5g | Sodium 79mg | Carbs 10.8g | Fiber 1.3g | Sugar 4.8g | Protein 2.3g

Savory Sweet Potato Hash

Servings: 6
Cooking Time: 18 Minutes
Ingredients:
- 2 medium sweet potatoes, peeled and cut into 1-inch cubes
- ½ green pepper, diced
- ½ red onion, diced
- 110 g baby mushrooms, diced
- 2 tablespoons olive oil
- 1 garlic clove, minced
- ½ teaspoon salt
- ½ teaspoon black pepper
- ½ tablespoon chopped fresh rosemary

Directions:
1. In a large bowl, toss all ingredients together until the vegetables are well coated and seasonings distributed.
2. Pour half of the vegetables into the zone 1 drawer and the rest into zone 2 drawer. In zone 1, select Roast button and adjust temperature to 190°C, set time to 18 minutes. In zone 2, select Match Cook and press Start.
3. Pause and toss or flip the vegetables once halfway through. Transfer to a serving bowl or individual plates and enjoy.

Banana And Raisins Muffins

Servings: 2
Cooking Time: 16
Ingredients:
- Salt, pinch
- 2 eggs, whisked
- 1/3 cup butter, melted
- 4 tablespoons of almond milk
- ¼ teaspoon of vanilla extract
- ½ teaspoon of baking powder
- 1-1/2 cup all-purpose flour
- 1 cup mashed bananas
- 2 tablespoons of raisins

Directions:
1. Take about 4 large (one-cup sized) ramekins and layer them with muffin papers.
2. Crack eggs in a large bowl, and whisk it all well and start adding vanilla extract, almond milk, baking powder, and melted butter
3. Whisk the ingredients very well.
4. Take a separate bowl and add the all-purpose flour, and salt.
5. Now, combine the add dry ingredients with the wet ingredients.
6. Now, pour mashed bananas and raisins into this batter
7. Mix it well to make a batter for the muffins.
8. Now pour the batter into four ramekins and divided the ramekins in the air fryer zones.
9. Set the timer for zone 1 to 16 minutes at 350 degrees F.
10. Select the MATCH button for the zone 2 basket.
11. Check if not done, and let it AIR FRY for one more minute.
12. Once it is done, serve.

Nutrition:
- (Per serving) Calories 727| Fat 43.1g| Sodium366 mg | Carbs 74.4g | Fiber 4.7g | Sugar 16.1g | Protein 14.1g

Breakfast Pitta

Servings: 2
Cooking Time: 6 Minutes
Ingredients:
- 1 wholemeal pitta
- 2 teaspoons olive oil
- ½ shallot, diced
- ¼ teaspoon garlic, minced
- 1 large egg
- ¼ teaspoon dried oregano
- ¼ teaspoon dried thyme
- ⅛ teaspoon salt
- 2 tablespoons shredded Parmesan cheese

Directions:
1. Brush the top of the pitta with olive oil, then spread the diced shallot and minced garlic over the pitta. Crack the egg into a small bowl or ramekin, and season it with oregano, thyme, and salt.
2. Place the pitta into the zone 1 drawer, and gently pour the egg onto the top of the pitta. Sprinkle with cheese over the top.
3. Select Bake button and adjust temperature to 190ºC, set time to 6 minutes and press Start. After the end, allow to cool for 5 minutes before cutting into pieces for serving.

Potatoes Lyonnaise

Servings: 4
Cooking Time: 31 Minutes
Ingredients:
- 1 sweet/mild onion, sliced
- 1 teaspoon butter, melted
- 1 teaspoon brown sugar
- 2 large white potatoes (about 450 g in total), sliced ½-inch thick
- 1 tablespoon vegetable oil
- Salt and freshly ground black pepper, to taste

Directions:
1. Preheat the air fryer to 188ºC.
2. Toss the sliced onions, melted butter and brown sugar together in the zone 1 air fryer drawer. Air fry for 8 minutes, shaking the drawer occasionally to help the onions cook evenly.
3. While the onions are cooking, bring a saucepan of salted water to a boil on the stovetop. Par-cook the potatoes in boiling water for 3 minutes. Drain the potatoes and pat them dry with a clean kitchen towel.
4. Add the potatoes to the onions in the zone 1 air fryer drawer and drizzle with vegetable oil. Toss to coat the potatoes with the oil and season with salt and freshly ground black pepper.
5. Increase the air fryer temperature to 204ºC and air fry for 20 minutes, tossing the vegetables a few times during the cooking time to help the potatoes brown evenly.
6. Season with salt and freshly ground black pepper and serve warm.

Jalapeño Popper Egg Cups And Cheddar Soufflés

Servings: 6
Cooking Time: 12 Minutes
Ingredients:
- Jalapeño Popper Egg Cups:
- 4 large eggs
- 60 ml chopped pickled jalapeños
- 60 g full-fat cream cheese
- 120 ml shredded sharp Cheddar cheese
- Cheddar Soufflés:
- 3 large eggs, whites and yolks separated
- ¼ teaspoon cream of tartar
- 120 ml shredded sharp Cheddar cheese
- 85 g cream cheese, softened

Directions:
1. Make the Jalapeño Popper Egg Cups :
2. In a medium bowl, beat the eggs, then pour into four silicone muffin cups.
3. In a large microwave-safe bowl, place jalapeños, cream cheese, and Cheddar. Microwave for 30 seconds and stir. Take a spoonful, approximately ¼ of the mixture, and place it in the center of one of the egg cups. Repeat with remaining mixture.
4. Place egg cups into the zone 1 air fryer drawer.
5. Adjust the temperature to 160°C and bake for 10 minutes.
6. Serve warm.
7. Make the Cheddar Soufflés :
8. In a large bowl, beat egg whites together with cream of tartar until soft peaks form, about 2 minutes.
9. In a separate medium bowl, beat egg yolks, Cheddar, and cream cheese together until frothy, about 1 minute. Add egg yolk mixture to whites, gently folding until combined.
10. Pour mixture evenly into four ramekins greased with cooking spray. Place ramekins into the zone 2 air fryer drawer. Adjust the temperature to 176°C and bake for 12 minutes. Eggs will be browned on the top and firm in the center when done. Serve warm.

Air Fried Bacon And Eggs

Servings: 1
Cooking Time: 10 Minutes
Ingredients:
- 2 eggs
- 2 slices bacon

Directions:
1. Grease a ramekin using cooking spray.
2. Install the crisper plate in the zone 1 drawer and place the bacon inside it. Insert the drawer into the unit.
3. Crack the eggs and add them to the greased ramekin.
4. Install the crisper plate in the zone 2 drawer and place the ramekin inside it. Insert the drawer into the unit.
5. Select zone 1 to AIR FRY for 9–11 minutes at 400 degrees F/ 200 degrees C. Select zone 2 to AIR FRY for 8–9 minutes at 350 degrees F/ 175 degrees C. Press SYNC.
6. Press START/STOP to begin cooking.
7. Enjoy!

Nutrition:
- (Per serving) Calories 331 | Fat 24.5g | Sodium 1001mg | Carbs 1.2g | Fiber 0g | Sugar 0.7g | Protein 25.3g

Savory Soufflé

Servings: 4
Cooking Time: 8 Minutes
Ingredients:
- 4 tablespoons light cream
- 4 eggs
- 2 tablespoons fresh parsley, chopped
- 2 fresh red chilies pepper, chopped
- Salt, as required

Directions:
1. In a bowl, add all the ingredients and beat until well combined.
2. Divide the mixture into 4 greased soufflé dishes.
3. Press either "Zone 1" and "Zone 2" of Tefal 2-Basket Air Fryer and then rotate the knob to select "Air Fry".
4. Set the temperature to 200 degrees C, and then set the time for 5 minutes to preheat.
5. After preheating, arrange soufflé dishes into the basket.
6. Slide basket into Air Fryer and set the time for 8 minutes.
7. After cooking time is completed, remove the soufflé dishes from Air Fryer and serve warm.

Turkey Ham Muffins

Servings: 16
Cooking Time: 10 Minutes
Ingredients:
- 1 egg
- 340g all-purpose flour
- 85g turkey ham, chopped
- 2 tbsp mix herbs, chopped
- 235g cheddar cheese, shredded
- 1 onion, chopped
- 2 tsp baking powder
- 2 tbsp butter, melted
- 237ml milk
- Pepper
- Salt

Directions:
1. In a large bowl, mix flour and baking powder.
2. Add egg, butter, and milk and mix until well combined.
3. Add herbs, cheese, onion, and turkey ham and mix well.
4. Insert a crisper plate in the Tefal air fryer baskets.
5. Pour the batter into the silicone muffin moulds.
6. Place muffin moulds in both baskets.
7. Select zone 1, then select "air fry" mode and set the temperature to 355 degrees F for 10 minutes. Press "match" to match zone 2 settings to zone 1. Press "start/stop" to begin.

Nutrition:
- (Per serving) Calories 140 | Fat 4.8g |Sodium 126mg | Carbs 18.2g | Fiber 0.7g | Sugar 1.2g | Protein 5.8g

Cauliflower Avocado Toast And All-in-one Toast

Servings: 3
Cooking Time: 10 Minutes
Ingredients:
- Cauliflower Avocado Toast:
- 1 (40 g) steamer bag cauliflower
- 1 large egg
- 120 ml shredded Mozzarella cheese
- 1 ripe medium avocado
- ½ teaspoon garlic powder
- ¼ teaspoon ground black pepper
- All-in-One Toast:
- 1 strip bacon, diced
- 1 slice 1-inch thick bread
- 1 egg
- Salt and freshly ground black pepper, to taste
- 60 ml grated Monterey Jack or Chedday cheese

Directions:
1. Make the Cauliflower Avocado Toast :
2. Cook cauliflower according to package instructions. Remove from bag and place into cheesecloth or clean towel to remove excess moisture.
3. Place cauliflower into a large bowl and mix in egg and Mozzarella. Cut a piece of parchment to fit your air fryer drawer. Separate the cauliflower mixture into two, and place it on the parchment in two mounds. Press out the cauliflower mounds into a ¼-inch-thick rectangle. Place the parchment into the zone 1 air fryer drawer.
4. Adjust the temperature to 204°C and set the timer for 8 minutes.
5. Flip the cauliflower halfway through the cooking time.
6. When the timer beeps, remove the parchment and allow the cauliflower to cool 5 minutes.
7. Cut open the avocado and remove the pit. Scoop out the inside, place it in a medium bowl, and mash it with garlic powder and pepper. Spread onto the cauliflower. Serve immediately.
8. Make the All-in-One Toast :
9. Preheat the zone 2 air fryer drawer to 204°C.
10. Air fry the bacon for 3 minutes, shaking the zone 2 drawer once or twice while it cooks. Remove the bacon to a paper towel lined plate and set aside.
11. Use a sharp paring knife to score a large circle in the middle of the slice of bread, cutting halfway through, but not all the way through to the cutting board. Press down on the circle in the center of the bread slice to create an indentation.
12. Transfer the slice of bread, hole side up, to the air fryer drawer. Crack the egg into the center of the bread, and season with salt and pepper.
13. Adjust the air fryer temperature to 192°C and air fry for 5 minutes. Sprinkle the grated cheese around the edges of the bread, leaving the center of the yolk uncovered, and top with the cooked bacon. Press the cheese and bacon into the bread lightly to help anchor it to the bread and prevent it from blowing around in the air fryer.
14. Air fry for one or two more minutes, just to melt the cheese and finish cooking the egg. Serve immediately.

Cinnamon Air Fryer Apples

Servings: 4
Cooking Time: 15 Minutes
Ingredients:
- 2 apples, cut in half and cored
- 2 tablespoons butter, melted
- 40g oats
- 3 teaspoons honey
- ½ teaspoon ground cinnamon

Directions:
1. Apply the butter to the apple halves' tops.
2. Combine the remaining butter, oats, honey, and cinnamon in a mixing bowl.
3. Distribute the mixture evenly over the apples' tops.
4. Press either "Zone 1" or "Zone 2" and then rotate the knob to select "Air Fryer".
5. Set the temperature to 190 degrees C, and then set the time for 3 minutes to preheat.
6. After preheating, Arrange the apples in the basket.
7. Slide basket into Air Fryer and set the time for 15 minutes.
8. After cooking time is completed, remove basket from Air Fryer.
9. Place them on serving plates and serve.

Breakfast Sammies

Servings: 5
Cooking Time: 20 Minutes
Ingredients:
- Biscuits:
- 6 large egg whites
- 475 ml blanched almond flour, plus more if needed
- 1½ teaspoons baking powder
- ½ teaspoon fine sea salt
- 60 ml (½ stick) very cold unsalted butter (or lard for dairy-free), cut into ¼-inch pieces
- Eggs:
- 5 large eggs
- ½ teaspoon fine sea salt
- ¼ teaspoon ground black pepper
- 5 (30 g) slices Cheddar cheese (omit for dairy-free)
- 10 thin slices ham

Directions:
1. Spray the two air fryer drawers with avocado oil. Preheat the air fryer to 176°C. Grease two pie pans or two baking pans that will fit inside your air fryer. 2. Make the biscuits: In a medium-sized bowl, whip the egg whites with a hand mixer until very stiff. Set aside. 3. In a separate medium-sized bowl, stir together the almond flour, baking powder, and salt until well combined. Cut in the butter. Gently fold the flour mixture into the egg whites with a rubber spatula. If the dough is too wet to form into mounds, add a few tablespoons of almond flour until the dough holds together well. 4. Using a large spoon, divide the dough into 5 equal portions and drop them about 1 inch apart on one of the greased pie pans. Place the pan in the two air fryer drawers and bake for 11 to 14 minutes, until the biscuits are golden brown. Remove from the air fryer and set aside to cool. 5. Make the eggs: Set the air fryer to 192°C. Crack the eggs into the remaining greased pie pan and sprinkle with the salt and pepper. Place the eggs in the air fryer to bake for 5 minutes, or until they are cooked to your liking. 6. Open the air fryer and top each egg yolk with a slice of cheese. Bake for another minute, or until the cheese is melted. 7. Once the biscuits are cool, slice them in half lengthwise. Place 1 cooked egg topped with cheese and 2 slices of ham in each biscuit. 8. Store leftover biscuits, eggs, and ham in separate airtight containers in the fridge for up to 3 days. Reheat the biscuits and eggs on a baking sheet in a preheated 176°C air fryer for 5 minutes, or until warmed through.

Cheesy Baked Eggs

Servings: 4
Cooking Time: 16 Minutes
Ingredients:
- 4 large eggs
- 57g smoked gouda, shredded
- Everything bagel seasoning, to taste
- Salt and pepper to taste

Directions:
1. Crack one egg in each ramekin.
2. Top the egg with bagel seasoning, black pepper, salt and gouda.
3. Place 2 ramekins in each air fryer basket.
4. Return the air fryer basket 1 to Zone 1, and basket 2 to Zone 2 of the Tefal 2-Basket Air Fryer.
5. Choose the "Air Fry" mode for Zone 1 and set the temperature to 400 degrees F and 16 minutes of cooking time.
6. Select the "MATCH COOK" option to copy the settings for Zone 2.
7. Initiate cooking by pressing the START/PAUSE BUTTON.
8. Serve warm.

Nutrition:
- (Per serving) Calories 190 | Fat 18g | Sodium 150mg | Carbs 0.6g | Fiber 0.4g | Sugar 0.4g | Protein 7.2g

Sausage Hash And Baked Eggs

Servings: 4
Cooking Time: 30 Minutes
Ingredients:
- FOR THE HASH
- 2 yellow potatoes (about 1 pound), cut into ½-inch pieces
- 4 garlic cloves, minced
- 1 teaspoon kosher salt
- ¼ teaspoon freshly ground black pepper
- 2 tablespoons olive oil
- ½ pound pork breakfast sausage meat
- 1 small yellow onion, diced
- 1 red bell pepper, diced
- 1 teaspoon Italian seasoning
- FOR THE EGGS
- Nonstick cooking spray
- 4 large eggs
- 4 tablespoons water

Directions:
1. To prep the hash: In a large bowl, combine the potatoes, garlic, salt, black pepper, and olive oil and toss to coat. Crumble in the sausage and mix until combined.
2. To prep the eggs: Mist 4 silicone muffin cups with cooking spray. Crack 1 egg into each muffin cup. Top each egg with 1 tablespoon of water.
3. To cook the hash and eggs: Install a crisper plate in the Zone 1 basket. Place the sausage and potato mixture in the Zone 1 basket and insert the basket in the unit. Place the egg cups in the Zone 2 basket and insert the basket in the unit.
4. Select Zone 1, select AIR FRY, set the temperature to 400°F, and set the time to 30 minutes.
5. Select Zone 2, select BAKE, set the temperature to 325°F, and set the time to 12 minutes. Select SMART FINISH.
6. Press START/PAUSE to begin cooking.
7. When the Zone 1 timer reads 20 minutes, press START/PAUSE. Remove the basket and add the onion, bell pepper, and Italian seasoning to the hash. Mix until combined, breaking up any large pieces of sausage. Reinsert the basket and press START/PAUSE to resume cooking.
8. When cooking is complete, serve the hash topped with an egg.

Nutrition:
- (Per serving) Calories: 400; Total fat: 23g; Saturated fat: 5.5g; Carbohydrates: 31g; Fiber: 2g; Protein: 19g; Sodium: 750mg

Jelly Doughnuts

Servings: 4
Cooking Time: 6 Minutes
Ingredients:
- 1 package Pillsbury Grands
- ½ cup seedless raspberry jelly
- 1 tablespoon butter, melted
- ½ cup sugar

Directions:
1. Spread the Pillsbury dough and cut out 3 inches round doughnuts out of it.
2. Place the doughnuts in the air fryer baskets and brush them with butter.
3. Drizzle sugar over the doughnuts.
4. Return the air fryer basket 1 to Zone 1, and basket 2 to Zone 2 of the Tefal 2-Basket Air Fryer.
5. Choose the "Air Fry" mode for Zone 1 at 320 degrees F and 6 minutes of cooking time.
6. Select the "MATCH COOK" option to copy the settings for Zone 2.
7. Initiate cooking by pressing the START/PAUSE BUTTON.
8. Use a piping bag to inject raspberry jelly into each doughnut.
9. Serve.

Nutrition:
- (Per serving) Calories 102 | Fat 7.6g | Sodium 545mg | Carbs 1.5g | Fiber 0.4g | Sugar 0.7g | Protein 7.1g

Snacks And Appetizers Recipes

Tasty Sweet Potato Wedges

Servings: 4
Cooking Time: 20 Minutes
Ingredients:
- 2 sweet potatoes, peel & cut into wedges
- 1 tbsp BBQ spice rub
- ½ tsp sweet paprika
- 1 tbsp olive oil
- Pepper
- Salt

Directions:
1. In a bowl, toss sweet potato wedges with sweet paprika, oil, BBQ spice rub, pepper, and salt.
2. Insert a crisper plate in the Tefal air fryer baskets.
3. Add sweet potato wedges in both baskets.
4. Select zone 1 then select "air fry" mode and set the temperature to 390 degrees F for 20 minutes. Press "match" to match zone 2 settings to zone 1. Press "start/stop" to begin. Turn halfway through.

Pumpkin Fries

Servings: 4
Cooking Time: 15 Minutes
Ingredients:
- 120g plain Greek yoghurt
- 2 to 3 teaspoons minced chipotle peppers
- ⅛ teaspoon plus ½ teaspoon salt, divided
- 1 medium pie pumpkin
- ¼ teaspoon garlic powder
- ¼ teaspoon ground cumin
- ¼ teaspoon chili powder
- ¼ teaspoon pepper

Directions:
1. Combine yoghurt, chipotle peppers, and ⅛ teaspoon salt in a small bowl. Refrigerate until ready to serve, covered.
2. Peeled the pumpkin and split it in half lengthwise. Discard the seeds. Cut pumpkin into 1 cm strips.
3. Place in a large mixing bowl. Toss with ½ teaspoon salt, garlic powder, cumin, chili powder, and pepper.
4. Press either "Zone 1" or "Zone 2" and then rotate the knob to select "Air Fry".
5. Set the temperature to 200 degrees C, and then set the time for 5 minutes to preheat.
6. After preheating, spray the Air-Fryer basket with cooking spray and line with parchment paper. Arrange pumpkin fries and spritz cooking spray on them.
7. Slide the basket into the Air Fryer and set the time for 8 minutes.
8. After that, toss them and again cook for 3 minutes longer.
9. After cooking time is completed, transfer them onto serving plates and serve.

JTater Tots

Servings: 4
Cooking Time: 8 Minutes
Ingredients:
- 16 ounces tater tots
- ½ cup shredded cheddar cheese
- 1½ teaspoons bacon bits
- 2 green onions, chopped
- Sour cream (optional)

Directions:
1. Place a crisper plate in each drawer. Put the tater tots into the drawers in a single layer. Insert the drawers into the unit.
2. Select zone 1, then AIR FRY, then set the temperature to 360 degrees F/ 180 degrees C with a 6-minute timer. To match zone 2 settings to zone 1, choose MATCH. To begin, select START/STOP.
3. When the cooking time is over, add the shredded cheddar cheese, bacon bits, and green onions over the tater tots. Select zone 1, AIR FRY, 360 degrees F/ 180 degrees C, for 4 minutes. Select MATCH. Press START/STOP.
4. Drizzle sour cream over the top before serving.
5. Enjoy!

Nutrition:
- (Per serving) Calories 335 | Fat 19.1g | Sodium 761mg | Carbs 34.1g | Fiber 3g | Sugar 0.6g | Protein 8.9g

Jalapeño Poppers And Greek Potato Skins With Olives And Feta

Servings: 8
Cooking Time: 45 Minutes
Ingredients:
- Jalapeño Poppers:
- Oil, for spraying
- 227 g soft white cheese
- 177 ml gluten-free breadcrumbs, divided
- 2 tablespoons chopped fresh parsley
- ½ teaspoon granulated garlic
- ½ teaspoon salt
- 10 jalapeño peppers, halved and seeded
- Greek Potato Skins with Olives and Feta:
- 2 russet or Maris Piper potatoes
- 3 tablespoons olive oil, divided, plus more for drizzling (optional)
- 1 teaspoon rock salt, divided
- ¼ teaspoon black pepper
- 2 tablespoons fresh coriander, chopped, plus more for serving
- 60 ml Kalamata olives, diced
- 60 ml crumbled feta
- Chopped fresh parsley, for garnish (optional)

Directions:
1. Make the Jalapeño Popper s: Line the zone 1 air fryer basket with parchment and spray lightly with oil.
2. In a medium bowl, mix together the soft white cheese, half of the breadcrumbs, the parsley, garlic, and salt. 3. Spoon the mixture into the jalapeño halves. Gently press the stuffed jalapeños in the remaining breadcrumbs. 4. Place the stuffed jalapeños in the prepared basket. 5. Air fry at 190°C for 20 minutes, or until the cheese is melted and the breadcrumbs are crisp and golden brown.
2. Make the Greek Potato Skins with Olives and Feta :
3. Preheat the air fryer to 190°C.
4. Using a fork, poke 2 to 3 holes in the potatoes, then coat each with about ½ tablespoon olive oil and ½ teaspoon salt.
5. Place the potatoes into the zone 2 air fryer basket and bake for 30 minutes.
6. Remove the potatoes from the air fryer, and slice in half. Using a spoon, scoop out the flesh of the potatoes, leaving a ½-inch layer of potato inside the skins, and set the skins aside.
7. In a medium bowl, combine the scooped potato middles with the remaining 2 tablespoons of olive oil, ½ teaspoon of salt, black pepper, and coriander. Mix until well combined.
8. Divide the potato filling into the now-empty potato skins, spreading it evenly over them. Top each potato with a tablespoon each of the olives and feta.
9. Place the loaded potato skins back into the air fryer and bake for 15 minutes.
10. Serve with additional chopped coriander or parsley and a drizzle of olive oil, if desired.

Stuffed Mushrooms

Servings: 5
Cooking Time: 8 Minutes
Ingredients:
- 8 ounces fresh mushrooms (I used Monterey)
- 4 ounces cream cheese
- ¼ cup shredded parmesan cheese
- ⅛ cup shredded sharp cheddar cheese
- ⅛ cup shredded white cheddar cheese
- 1 teaspoon Worcestershire sauce
- 2 garlic cloves, minced
- Salt and pepper, to taste

Directions:
1. To prepare the mushrooms for stuffing, remove their stems. Make a circle cut around the area where the stem used to be. Continue to cut until all of the superfluous mushroom is removed.
2. To soften the cream cheese, microwave it for 15 seconds.
3. Combine the cream cheese, shredded cheeses, salt, pepper, garlic, and Worcestershire sauce in a medium mixing bowl. To blend, stir everything together.
4. Stuff the mushrooms with the cheese mixture.
5. Place a crisper plate in each drawer. Put the stuffed mushrooms in a single layer in each drawer. Insert the drawers into the unit.
6. Select zone 1, then AIR FRY, then set the temperature to 360 degrees F/ 180 degrees C with an 8-minute timer. To match zone 2 settings to zone 1, choose MATCH. To begin, select START/STOP.
7. Serve and enjoy!

Nutrition:
- (Per serving) Calories 230 | Fat 9.5g | Sodium 105mg | Carbs 35.5g | Fiber 5.1g | Sugar 0.1g | Protein 7.1g

"fried" Ravioli With Zesty Marinara

Servings: 6
Cooking Time: 20 Minutes

Ingredients:
- FOR THE RAVIOLI
- ¼ cup all-purpose flour
- 1 large egg
- 1 tablespoon water
- ⅔ cup Italian-style bread crumbs
- 1 pound frozen cheese ravioli, thawed
- Nonstick cooking spray
- FOR THE MARINARA
- 1 (28-ounce) can chunky crushed tomatoes with basil and oregano
- 1 tablespoon unsalted butter
- 2 garlic cloves, minced
- ¼ teaspoon kosher salt
- ¼ teaspoon red pepper flakes

Directions:
1. To prep the ravioli: Set up a breading station with three small shallow bowls. Put the flour in the first bowl. In the second bowl, beat the egg and water. Place the bread crumbs in the third bowl.
2. Bread the ravioli in this order: First dip them into the flour, coating both sides. Then dip into the beaten egg. Finally, coat them in the bread crumbs, gently pressing the crumbs into the ravioli to help them stick.
3. Mist both sides of the ravioli generously with cooking spray.
4. To prep the marinara: In the Zone 2 basket, combine the crushed tomatoes, butter, garlic, salt, and red pepper flakes.
5. To cook the ravioli and sauce: Install a crisper plate in the Zone 1 basket and add the ravioli to the basket. Insert the basket in the unit. Insert the Zone 2 basket in the unit.
6. Select Zone 1, select AIR FRY, set the temperature to 390°F, and set the time to 20 minutes.
7. Select Zone 2, select BAKE, set the temperature to 350°F, and set the time to 15 minutes. Select SMART FINISH.
8. Press START/PAUSE to begin cooking.
9. When the Zone 1 timer reads 7 minutes, press START/PAUSE. Remove the basket and shake to redistribute the ravioli. Reinsert the basket and press START/PAUSE to resume cooking.
10. When cooking is complete, the breading will be crisp and golden brown. Transfer the ravioli to a plate and the marinara to a bowl. Serve hot.

Nutrition:
- (Per serving) Calories: 282; Total fat: 8g; Saturated fat: 3g; Carbohydrates: 39g; Fiber: 4.5g; Protein: 13g; Sodium: 369mg

Pretzels

Servings: 8
Cooking Time: 6 Minutes

Ingredients:
- 360ml warm water
- 1 tablespoon dry active yeast
- 1 tablespoon sugar
- 1 tablespoon olive oil
- 500g plain flour
- 1 teaspoon salt
- 1 large egg
- 1 tablespoon water

Directions:
1. Combine warm water, yeast, sugar, and olive oil in a large mixing bowl. Stir everything together and leave aside for about 5 minutes.
2. Add 375g flour and a teaspoon of salt to the mixture. Stir well.
3. On a floured surface, roll out the dough. Knead for 3 to 5 minutes, or until the dough is no longer sticky, adding flour 1 tablespoon at a time if necessary.
4. The dough should be divided in half. At a time, work with half of the dough.
5. Each dough half should be divided into eight pieces.
6. Make a 45cm rope out of the dough. Make a U shape out of the dough. Twist the ends two more times.
7. Fold the ends of the dough over the spherical portion.
8. In a small mixing dish, whisk the egg and a tablespoon of water.
9. Brush the egg wash on both sides of the pretzel dough.
10. Press your chosen zone - "Zone 1" or "Zone 2" and then rotate the knob to select "Air Fryer".
11. Set the temperature to 185 degrees C, and then set the time for 5 minutes to preheat.
12. After preheating, arrange pretzels into the basket of each zone.
13. Slide the baskets into Air Fryer and set the time for 6 minutes.
14. After cooking time is completed, place on a wire rack for a few minutes, then transfer onto serving plates and serve.

Avocado Fries With Sriracha Dip

Servings: 4
Cooking Time: 6 Minutes
Ingredients:
- Avocado Fries
- 4 avocados, peeled and cut into sticks
- ¾ cup panko breadcrumbs
- ¼ cup flour
- 2 eggs, beaten
- ½ teaspoon garlic powder
- ½ teaspoon salt
- SRIRACHA-RANCH SAUCE
- ¼ cup ranch dressing
- 1 teaspoon sriracha sauce

Directions:
1. Mix flour with garlic powder and salt in a bowl.
2. Dredge the avocado sticks through the flour mixture.
3. Dip them in the eggs and coat them with breadcrumbs.
4. Place the coated fries in the air fryer baskets.
5. Return the air fryer basket 1 to Zone 1, and basket 2 to Zone 2 of the Tefal 2-Basket Air Fryer.
6. Choose the "Air Fry" mode for Zone 1 at 400 degrees F and 6 minutes of cooking time.
7. Select the "MATCH COOK" option to copy the settings for Zone 2.
8. Initiate cooking by pressing the START/PAUSE BUTTON.
9. Flip the fries once cooked halfway through.
10. Mix all the dipping sauce ingredients in a bowl.
11. Serve the fries with dipping sauce.

Crispy Tortilla Chips

Servings: 8
Cooking Time: 13 Minutes.
Ingredients:
- 4 (6-inch) corn tortillas
- 1 tablespoon Avocado Oil
- Sea salt to taste
- Cooking spray

Directions:
1. Spread the corn tortillas on the working surface.
2. Slice them into bite-sized triangles.
3. Toss them with salt and cooking oil.
4. Divide the triangles in the two crisper plates into a single layer.
5. Return the crisper plates to the Tefal Dual Zone Air Fryer.
6. Choose the Air Fry mode for Zone 1 and set the temperature to 390 degrees F and the time to 13 minutes.
7. Select the "MATCH" button to copy the settings for Zone 2.
8. Initiate cooking by pressing the START/STOP button.
9. Toss the chips once cooked halfway through, then resume cooking.
10. Serve and enjoy.

Nutrition:
- (Per serving) Calories 103 | Fat 8.4g |Sodium 117mg | Carbs 3.5g | Fiber 0.9g | Sugar 1.5g | Protein 5.1g

Mozzarella Arancini

Servings: 16 Arancini
Cooking Time: 8 To 11 Minutes
Ingredients:
- 475 ml cooked rice, cooled
- 2 eggs, beaten
- 355 ml panko breadcrumbs, divided
- 120 ml grated Parmesan cheese
- 2 tablespoons minced fresh basil
- 16 ¾-inch cubes Mozzarella cheese
- 2 tablespoons olive oil

Directions:
1. Preheat the air fryer to 205°C.
2. In a medium bowl, combine the rice, eggs, 120 ml of the breadcrumbs, Parmesan cheese, and basil. Form this mixture into 16 1½-inch balls.
3. Poke a hole in each of the balls with your finger and insert a Mozzarella cube. Form the rice mixture firmly around the cheese.
4. On a shallow plate, combine the remaining 240 ml of the breadcrumbs with the olive oil and mix well. Roll the rice balls in the breadcrumbs to coat.
5. Air fry the arancini in two baskets for 8 to 11 minutes or until golden brown.
6. Serve hot.

Stuffed Bell Peppers

Servings: 3
Cooking Time: 16
Ingredients:
- 6 large bell peppers
- 1-1/2 cup cooked rice
- 2 cups cheddar cheese

Directions:
1. Cut the bell peppers in half lengthwise and remove all the seeds.
2. Fill the cavity of each bell pepper with cooked rice.
3. Divide the bell peppers amongst the two zones of the air fryer basket.
4. Set the time for zone 1 for 200 degrees for 10 minutes.
5. Select MATCH button of zone 2 basket.
6. Afterward, take out the baskets and sprinkle cheese on top.
7. Set the time for zone 1 for 200 degrees for 6 minutes.
8. Select MATCH button of zone 2 basket.
9. Once it's done, serve.

Nutrition:
- (Per serving) Calories 605| Fat 26g | Sodium477 mg | Carbs68.3 g | Fiber4 g| Sugar 12.5g | Protein25.6 g

Crab Cakes

Servings: 4
Cooking Time: 15 Minutes
Ingredients:
- 227g lump crab meat
- 1 red capsicum, chopped
- 3 green onions, chopped
- 3 tablespoons mayonnaise
- 3 tablespoons breadcrumbs
- 2 teaspoons old bay seasoning
- 1 teaspoon lemon juice

Directions:
1. Mix crab meat with capsicum, onions and the rest of the ingredients in a food processor.
2. Make 4 inch crab cakes out of this mixture.
3. Divide the crab cakes into the Tefal 2 Baskets Air Fryer baskets.
4. Return the air fryer basket 1 to Zone 1, and basket 2 to Zone 2 of the Tefal 2-Basket Air Fryer.
5. Choose the "Air Fry" mode for Zone 1 at 370 degrees F and 10 minutes of cooking time.
6. Select the "MATCH COOK" option to copy the settings for Zone 2.
7. Initiate cooking by pressing the START/PAUSE BUTTON.
8. Flip the crab cakes once cooked halfway through.
9. Serve warm.

Bacon-wrapped Dates Bacon-wrapped Scallops

Servings: 6
Cooking Time: 12 Minutes
Ingredients:
- FOR THE SCALLOPS
- 6 slices bacon, halved crosswise
- 12 large sea scallops, patted dry
- FOR THE DATES
- 4 slices bacon, cut into thirds
- 12 pitted dates

Directions:
1. To prep the dates: Wrap each piece of bacon around a date and secure with a toothpick.
2. To cook the dates and the bacon for the scallops: Install a crisper plate in each of the two baskets. Place the bacon for the scallops in the Zone 1 basket in a single layer and insert the basket in the unit. Place the bacon-wrapped dates in the Zone 2 basket in a single layer and insert the basket in the unit.
3. Select Zone 1, select AIR FRY, set the temperature to 400°F, and set the time to 12 minutes.
4. Select Zone 2, select AIR FRY, set the temperature to 360°F, and set the time to 10 minutes. Select SMART FINISH.
5. Press START/PAUSE to begin cooking.
6. When the Zone 1 timer reads 9 minutes, press START/PAUSE. Remove the basket from the unit. Wrap each piece of bacon around a scallop and secure with a toothpick. Place the bacon-wrapped scallops in the basket. Reinsert the basket and press START/PAUSE to resume cooking.
7. When the Zone 1 timer reads 4 minutes, press START/PAUSE. Remove the basket and use silicone-tipped tongs to flip the scallops. Reinsert the basket and press START/PAUSE to resume cooking.
8. When cooking is complete, the scallops will be opaque and the bacon around both the scallops and dates will be crisp. Arrange the bacon-wrapped scallops and dates on a serving platter. Serve warm.

Nutrition:
- (Per serving) Calories: 191; Total fat: 2.5g; Saturated fat: 1g; Carbohydrates: 39g; Fiber: 4g; Protein: 3g; Sodium: 115mg

Taco-spiced Chickpeas And Black Bean Corn Dip

Servings: 7
Cooking Time: 17 Minutes
Ingredients:
- Taco-Spiced Chickpeas:
- Oil, for spraying
- 1 (439 g) can chickpeas, drained
- 1 teaspoon chilli powder
- ½ teaspoon ground cumin
- ½ teaspoon salt
- ½ teaspoon granulated garlic
- 2 teaspoons lime juice
- Black Bean Corn Dip:
- ½ (425 g) can black beans, drained and rinsed
- ½ (425 g) can corn, drained and rinsed
- 60 ml chunky salsa
- 57 g low-fat soft white cheese
- 60 ml shredded low-fat Cheddar cheese
- ½ teaspoon ground cumin
- ½ teaspoon paprika
- Salt and freshly ground black pepper, to taste

Directions:
1. Make the Taco-Spiced Chickpeas :
2. Line the zone 1 air fryer basket with parchment and spray lightly with oil. Place the chickpeas in the prepared basket.
3. Air fry at 200°C for 17 minutes, shaking or stirring the chickpeas and spraying lightly with oil every 5 to 7 minutes.
4. In a small bowl, mix together the chilli powder, cumin, salt, and garlic.
5. When 2 to 3 minutes of cooking time remain, sprinkle half of the seasoning mix over the chickpeas. Finish cooking.
6. Transfer the chickpeas to a medium bowl and toss with the remaining seasoning mix and the lime juice. Serve immediately.
7. Make the Black Bean Corn Dip :
8. Preheat the air fryer to 165°C.
9. In a medium bowl, mix together the black beans, corn, salsa, soft white cheese, Cheddar cheese, cumin, and paprika. Season with salt and pepper and stir until well combined.
10. Spoon the mixture into a baking dish.
11. Place baking dish in the zone 2 air fryer basket and bake until heated through, about 10 minutes.
12. Serve hot.

Miso-glazed Shishito Peppers Charred Lemon Shishito Peppers

Servings:4
Cooking Time: 10 Minutes
Ingredients:
- FOR THE MISO-GLAZED PEPPERS
- 2 tablespoons vegetable oil
- 2 tablespoons water
- 1 tablespoon white miso
- 1 teaspoon grated fresh ginger
- ½ pound shishito peppers
- FOR THE CHARRED LEMON PEPPERS
- ½ pound shishito peppers
- 1 lemon, cut into ⅛-inch-thick rounds
- 2 garlic cloves, minced
- 2 tablespoons vegetable oil
- ½ teaspoon kosher salt

Directions:
1. To prep the miso-glazed peppers: In a large bowl, mix the vegetable oil, water, miso, and ginger until well combined. Add the shishitos and toss to coat.
2. To prep the charred lemon peppers: In a large bowl, combine the shishitos, lemon slices, garlic, vegetable oil, and salt. Toss to coat.
3. To cook the peppers: Install a crisper plate in each of the two baskets. Place the miso-glazed peppers in the Zone 1 basket and insert the basket in the unit. Place the peppers with lemons in the Zone 2 basket and insert the basket in the unit.
4. Select Zone 1, select AIR FRY, set the temperature to 390°F, and set the time to 10 minutes. Select MATCH COOK to match Zone 2 settings to Zone 1.
5. Press START/PAUSE to begin cooking.
6. When both timers read 4 minutes, press START/PAUSE. Remove both baskets and shake well. Reinsert the baskets and press START/PAUSE to resume cooking.
7. When cooking is complete, serve immediately.

Nutrition:
- (Per serving) Calories: 165; Total fat: 14g; Saturated fat: 2g; Carbohydrates: 9g; Fiber: 2g; Protein: 2g; Sodium: 334mg

Mozzarella Sticks

Servings: 6
Cooking Time: 6 Minutes
Ingredients:
- 150g block Mozzarella cheese or string cheese
- 6 slices of white bread
- 1 large egg
- 1 tablespoon water
- 55g panko breadcrumbs
- 1 tablespoon olive oil

Directions:
1. Remove the crust from the bread. Discard or save for breadcrumbs.
2. Roll the bread into thin slices with a rolling pin.
3. Slice mozzarella into 30 cm x 10 cm -long sticks, nearly the same size as your bread slices.
4. In a small bowl, whisk together the egg and the water.
5. Fill a shallow pie plate halfway with panko.
6. Wrap a bread slice around each mozzarella stick.
7. Brush the egg wash around the edge of the bread and push to seal it. Brush all over the bread outside.
8. Dredge in Panko and push to coat on all sides.
9. Line basket with parchment paper.
10. Press either "Zone 1" or "Zone 2" and then rotate the knob to select "Air Fryer".
11. Set the temperature to 200 degrees C, and then set the time for 5 minutes to preheat.
12. After preheating, arrange sticks into the basket.
13. Slide the basket into the Air Fryer and set the time for 6 minutes.
14. After cooking time is completed, place on a wire rack for a few minutes, then transfer onto serving plates and serve.

Beef Jerky Pineapple Jerky

Servings: 8
Cooking Time: 6 To 12 Hours
Ingredients:
- FOR THE BEEF JERKY
- ½ cup reduced-sodium soy sauce
- ¼ cup pineapple juice
- 1 tablespoon dark brown sugar
- 1 tablespoon Worcestershire sauce
- ½ teaspoon smoked paprika
- ¼ teaspoon freshly ground black pepper
- ¼ teaspoon red pepper flakes
- 1 pound beef bottom round, trimmed of excess fat, cut into ¼-inch-thick slices
- FOR THE PINEAPPLE JERKY
- 1 pound pineapple, cut into ⅛-inch-thick rounds, pat dry
- 1 teaspoon chili powder (optional)

Directions:
1. To prep the beef jerky: In a large zip-top bag, combine the soy sauce, pineapple juice, brown sugar, Worcestershire sauce, smoked paprika, black pepper, and red pepper flakes.
2. Add the beef slices, seal the bag, and toss to coat the meat in the marinade. Refrigerate overnight or for at least 8 hours.
3. Remove the beef slices and discard the marinade. Using a paper towel, pat the slices dry to remove excess marinade.
4. To prep the pineapple jerky: Sprinkle the pineapple with chili powder (if using).
5. To dehydrate the jerky: Arrange half of the beef slices in a single layer in the Zone 1 basket, making sure they do not overlap. Place a crisper plate on top of the beef slices and arrange the remaining slices in a single layer on top of the crisper plate. Insert the basket in the unit.
6. Repeat this process with the pineapple in the Zone 2 basket and insert the basket in the unit.
7. Select Zone 1, select DEHYDRATE, set the temperature to 150°F, and set the time to 8 hours.
8. Select Zone 2, select DEHYDRATE, set the temperature to 135°F, and set the time to 12 hours.
9. Press START/PAUSE to begin cooking.
10. When the Zone 1 timer reads 2 hours, press START/PAUSE. Remove the basket and check the beef jerky for doneness. If necessary, reinsert the basket and press START/PAUSE to resume cooking.

Nutrition:
- (Per serving) Calories: 171; Total fat: 6.5g; Saturated fat: 2g; Carbohydrates: 2g; Fiber: 0g; Protein: 25g; Sodium: 369mg

Sausage Balls With Cheese

Servings: 8
Cooking Time: 10 To 11 Minutes
Ingredients:
- 340 g mild sausage meat
- 355 ml baking mix
- 240 ml shredded mild Cheddar cheese
- 85 g soft white cheese, at room temperature
- 1 to 2 tablespoons olive oil

Directions:
1. Preheat the air fryer to 165ºC. Line the two air fryer baskets with parchment paper.
2. Mix together the ground sausage, baking mix, Cheddar cheese, and soft white cheese in a large bowl and stir to incorporate.
3. Divide the sausage mixture into 16 equal portions and roll them into 1-inch balls with your hands.
4. Arrange the sausage balls on the parchment, leaving space between each ball.
5. Brush the sausage balls with the olive oil. Bake in the two baskets for 10 to 11 minutes, shaking the baskets halfway through, or until the balls are firm and lightly browned on both sides.
6. Remove from the baskets to a plate.
7. Serve warm.

Crispy Plantain Chips

Servings: 4
Cooking Time: 20 Minutes.
Ingredients:
- 1 green plantain
- 1 teaspoon canola oil
- ½ teaspoon sea salt

Directions:
1. Peel and cut the plantains into long strips using a mandolin slicer.
2. Grease the crisper plates with ½ teaspoon of canola oil.
3. Toss the plantains with salt and remaining canola oil.
4. Divide these plantains in the two crisper plates.
5. Return the crisper plate to the Tefal Dual Zone Air Fryer.
6. Choose the Air Fry mode for Zone 1 and set the temperature to 350 degrees F and the time to 20 minutes.
7. Select the "MATCH" button to copy the settings for Zone 2.
8. Initiate cooking by pressing the START/STOP button.
9. Toss the plantains after 10 minutes and resume cooking.
10. Serve warm.

Nutrition:
- (Per serving) Calories 122 | Fat 1.8g | Sodium 794mg | Carbs 17g | Fiber 8.9g | Sugar 1.6g | Protein 14.9g

Fish And Seafood Recipes

Perfect Parmesan Salmon

Servings: 4
Cooking Time: 10 Minutes
Ingredients:
- 4 salmon fillets
- 1/4 cup parmesan cheese, shredded
- 1/4 tsp dried dill
- 1/2 tbsp Dijon mustard
- 4 tbsp mayonnaise
- 1 lemon juice
- Pepper
- Salt

Directions:
1. In a small bowl, mix cheese, dill, mustard, mayonnaise, lemon juice, pepper, and salt.
2. Place salmon fillets into the air fryer basket and brush with cheese mixture.
3. Cook salmon fillets at 400 F for 10 minutes.
4. Serve and enjoy.

Flavorful Salmon With Green Beans

Servings: 4
Cooking Time: 10 Minutes
Ingredients:
- 4 ounces green beans
- 1 tablespoon canola oil
- 4 (6-ounce) salmon fillets
- 1/3 cup prepared sesame-ginger sauce
- Kosher salt, to taste
- Black pepper, to taste

Directions:
1. Toss the green beans with a teaspoon each of salt and pepper in a large bowl.
2. Place a crisper plate in each drawer. Place the green beans in the zone 1 drawer and insert it into the unit. Place the salmon into the zone 2 drawer and place it into the unit.
3. Select zone 1, then AIR FRY, and set the temperature to 390 degrees F/ 200 degrees C with a 10-minute timer.
4. Select zone 2, then AIR FRY, and set the temperature to 390 degrees F/ 200 degrees C with a 15-minute timer. Select SYNC. To begin cooking, press the START/STOP button.
5. Press START/STOP to pause the unit when the zone 2 timer reaches 9 minutes. Remove the salmon from the drawer and toss it in the sesame-ginger sauce. To resume cooking, replace the drawer in the device and press START/STOP.
6. When cooking is complete, serve the salmon and green beans immediately.

Nutrition:
- (Per serving) Calories 305 | Fat 16g | Sodium 535mg | Carbs 8.7g | Fiber 1g | Sugar 6.4g | Protein 34.9g

Orange-mustard Glazed Salmon

Servings: 2
Cooking Time: 10 Minutes
Ingredients:
- 1 tablespoon orange marmalade
- 1/4 teaspoon grated orange zest plus 1 tablespoon juice
- 2 teaspoons whole-grain mustard
- 2 (230 g) skin-on salmon fillets, 1½ inches thick
- Salt and pepper, to taste
- Vegetable oil spray

Directions:
1. Preheat the zone 1 air fryer drawer to 204°C.
2. Make foil sling for air fryer drawer by folding 1 long sheet of aluminum foil so it is 4 inches wide. Lay sheet of foil widthwise across drawer, pressing foil into and up sides of drawer. Fold excess foil as needed so that edges of foil are flush with top of drawer. Lightly spray foil and drawer with vegetable oil spray.
3. Combine marmalade, orange zest and juice, and mustard in bowl. Pat salmon dry with paper towels and season with salt and pepper. Brush tops and sides of fillets evenly with glaze. Arrange fillets skin side down on sling in prepared drawer, spaced evenly apart. Air fry salmon until center is still translucent when checked with the tip of a paring knife and registers 52°C, 10 to 14 minutes, using sling to rotate fillets halfway through cooking.
4. Using the sling, carefully remove salmon from air fryer. Slide fish spatula along underside of fillets and transfer to individual serving plates, leaving skin behind. Serve.

Southwestern Fish Fillets

Servings: 4
Cooking Time: 16 Minutes
Ingredients:
- 455g trout fillets
- 1 tsp garlic powder
- 29g breadcrumbs
- 15ml olive oil
- 1 tsp chilli powder
- 1 tsp onion powder

Directions:
1. In a small bowl, mix breadcrumbs, garlic powder, onion powder, and chilli powder.
2. Brush fish fillets with oil and coat with breadcrumbs.
3. Insert a crisper plate in the Tefal air fryer baskets.
4. Place coated fish fillets in both baskets.
5. Select zone 1 then select "air fry" mode and set the temperature to 375 degrees F for 16 minutes. Press "match" and "start/stop" to begin.

Nutrition:
- (Per serving) Calories 272 | Fat 13.5g | Sodium 120mg | Carbs 5g | Fiber 0.6g | Sugar 0.7g | Protein 31.1g

Bacon-wrapped Shrimp

Servings: 8
Cooking Time: 10 Minutes
Ingredients:
- 24 jumbo raw shrimp, deveined with tail on, fresh or thawed from frozen
- 8 slices bacon, cut into thirds
- 1 tablespoon olive oil
- 1 teaspoon paprika
- 1–2 cloves minced garlic
- 1 tablespoon finely chopped fresh parsley

Directions:
1. Combine the olive oil, paprika, garlic, and parsley in a small bowl.
2. If necessary, peel the raw shrimp, leaving the tails on.
3. Add the shrimp to the oil mixture. Toss to coat well.
4. Wrap a piece of bacon around the middle of each shrimp and place seam-side down on a small baking dish.
5. Refrigerate for 30 minutes before cooking.
6. Place a crisper plate in each drawer. Put the shrimp in a single layer in each drawer. Insert the drawers into the unit.
7. Select zone 1, then AIR FRY, then set the temperature to 360 degrees F/ 180 degrees C with a 10-minute timer. To match zone 2 settings to zone 1, choose MATCH. To begin, select START/STOP.
8. Remove the shrimp from the drawers when the cooking time is over.

Nutrition:
- (Per serving) Calories 479 | Fat 15.7g | Sodium 949mg | Carbs 0.6g | Fiber 0.1g | Sugar 0g | Protein 76.1g

Sweet Tilapia Fillets

Servings: 4
Cooking Time: 14 Minutes
Ingredients:
- 2 tablespoons granulated sweetener
- 1 tablespoon apple cider vinegar
- 4 tilapia fillets, boneless
- 1 teaspoon olive oil

Directions:
1. Mix apple cider vinegar with olive oil and sweetener.
2. Then rub the tilapia fillets with the sweet mixture and put in the two air fryer drawers in one layer. Cook the fish at 182°C for 7 minutes per side.

Panko-crusted Fish Sticks

Servings: 4
Cooking Time: 15 Minutes
Ingredients:
- Tartar Sauce:
- 470 ml mayonnaise
- 2 tablespoons dill pickle relish
- 1 tablespoon dried minced onions
- Fish Sticks:
- Olive or vegetable oil, for spraying
- 455 g tilapia fillets
- 75 g plain flour
- 120 g panko bread crumbs
- 2 tablespoons Creole seasoning
- 2 teaspoons garlic granules
- 1 teaspoon onion powder
- ½ teaspoon salt
- ¼ teaspoon freshly ground black pepper
- 1 large egg

Directions:
1. Make the Tartar Sauce: In a small bowl, whisk together the mayonnaise, pickle relish, and onions. Cover with plastic wrap and refrigerate until ready to serve. You can make this sauce ahead of time; the flavors will intensify as it chills. Make the Fish Sticks: 2. Preheat the air fryer to 175°C. Line the two air fryer baskets with baking paper and spray lightly with oil. 3. Cut the fillets into equal-size sticks and place them in a zip-top plastic bag. 4. Add the flour to the bag, seal, and shake well until evenly coated. 5. In a shallow bowl, mix together the bread crumbs, Creole seasoning, garlic, onion powder, salt, and black pepper. 6. In a small bowl, whisk the egg. 7. Dip the fish sticks in the egg, then dredge in the bread crumb mixture until completely coated. 8. Place the fish sticks in the two prepared baskets. Do not overcrowd. Spray lightly with oil. 9. Cook for 12 to 15 minutes, or until browned and cooked through. Serve with the tartar sauce.

Cod With Avocado And Garlic Prawns

Servings: 5
Cooking Time: 10 Minutes
Ingredients:
- Cod with Avocado:
- 90 g shredded cabbage
- 60 ml full-fat sour cream
- 2 tablespoons full-fat mayonnaise
- 20 g chopped pickled jalapeños
- 2 (85 g) cod fillets
- 1 teaspoon chilli powder
- 1 teaspoon cumin
- ½ teaspoon paprika
- ¼ teaspoon garlic powder
- 1 medium avocado, peeled, pitted, and sliced
- ½ medium lime
- Garlic Prawns:
- Prawns:
- Olive or vegetable oil, for spraying
- 450 g medium raw prawns, peeled and deveined
- 6 tablespoons unsalted butter, melted
- 120 g panko bread crumbs
- 2 tablespoons garlic granules
- 1 teaspoon salt
- ½ teaspoon freshly ground black pepper
- Garlic Butter Sauce:
- 115 g unsalted butter
- 2 teaspoons garlic granules
- ¾ teaspoon salt (omit if using salted butter)

Directions:
1. Make the Cod with Avocado :
2. In a large bowl, place cabbage, sour cream, mayonnaise, and jalapeños. Mix until fully coated. Let sit for 20 minutes in the refrigerator.
3. Sprinkle cod fillets with chilli powder, cumin, paprika, and garlic powder. Place each fillet into the zone 1 air fryer drawer.
4. Adjust the temperature to 188°C and set the timer for 10 minutes.
5. Flip the fillets halfway through the cooking time. When fully cooked, fish should have an internal temperature of at least 64°C.
6. To serve, divide slaw mixture into two serving bowls, break cod fillets into pieces and spread over the bowls, and top with avocado. Squeeze lime juice over each bowl. Serve immediately.
7. Make the Garlic Prawns :
8. Make the Prawns
9. Preheat the air fryer to 204°C. Line the zone 2 air fryer drawer with baking paper and spray lightly with oil.
10. Place the prawns and melted butter in a zip-top plastic bag, seal, and shake well, until evenly coated.
11. In a medium bowl, mix together the breadcrumbs, garlic, salt, and black pepper.
12. Add the prawns to the panko mixture and toss until evenly coated. Shake off any excess coating.
13. Place the prawns in the prepared drawer and spray lightly with oil.
14. Cook for 8 to 10 minutes, flipping and spraying with oil after 4 to 5 minutes, until golden brown and crispy. Make the Garlic Butter Sauce
15. In a microwave-safe bowl, combine the butter, garlic, and salt and microwave on 50% power for 30 to 60 seconds, stirring every 15 seconds, until completely melted.
16. Serve the prawns immediately with the garlic butter sauce on the side for dipping.

Tasty Parmesan Shrimp

Servings: 6
Cooking Time: 10minutes
Ingredients:
- 908g cooked shrimp, peeled & deveined
- ½ tsp oregano
- 59g parmesan cheese, grated
- 1 tbsp garlic, minced
- 30ml olive oil
- 1 tsp onion powder
- 1 tsp basil
- Pepper
- Salt

Directions:
1. Toss shrimp with oregano, cheese, garlic, oil, onion powder, basil, pepper, and salt in a bowl.
2. Insert a crisper plate in the Tefal air fryer baskets.
3. Add the shrimp mixture to both baskets.
4. Select zone 1, then select "air fry" mode and set the temperature to 360 degrees F for 10 minutes. Press "match" to match zone 2 settings to zone 1. Press "start/stop" to begin.

Nutrition:
- (Per serving) Calories 224 | Fat 7.3g |Sodium 397mg | Carbs 3.2g | Fiber 0.1g | Sugar 0.2g | Protein 34.6g

Herb Tuna Patties

Servings: 10
Cooking Time: 12 Minutes
Ingredients:
- 2 eggs
- 425g can tuna, drained & diced
- ½ tsp garlic powder
- ½ small onion, minced
- 1 celery stalk, chopped
- 42g parmesan cheese, grated
- 50g breadcrumbs
- ½ tsp dried oregano
- ½ tsp dried basil
- ½ tsp dried thyme
- 15ml lemon juice
- 1 lemon zest
- Pepper
- Salt

Directions:
1. In a bowl, mix tuna with remaining ingredients until well combined.
2. Insert a crisper plate in the Tefal air fryer baskets.
3. Make patties from the tuna mixture and place them in both baskets.
4. Select zone 1, then select "bake" mode and set the temperature to 380 degrees F for 12 minutes. Press "match" to match zone 2 settings to zone 1. Press "start/stop" to begin. Turn halfway through.

Nutrition:
- (Per serving) Calories 86 | Fat 1.5g |Sodium 90mg | Carbs 4.5g | Fiber 0.4g | Sugar 0.6g | Protein 12.8g

Herb Lemon Mussels

Servings: 6
Cooking Time: 10 Minutes
Ingredients:
- 1kg mussels, steamed & half shell
- 1 tbsp thyme, chopped
- 1 tbsp parsley, chopped
- 1 tsp dried parsley
- 1 tsp garlic, minced
- 60ml olive oil
- 45ml lemon juice
- Pepper
- Salt

Directions:
1. In a bowl, mix mussels with the remaining ingredients.
2. Insert a crisper plate in the Tefal air fryer baskets.
3. Add the mussels to both baskets.
4. Select zone 1 then select "air fry" mode and set the temperature to 360 degrees F for 10 minutes. Press "match" to match zone 2 settings to zone 1. Press "start/stop" to begin.

Nutrition:
- (Per serving) Calories 206 | Fat 11.9g |Sodium 462mg | Carbs 6.3g | Fiber 0.3g | Sugar 0.2g | Protein 18.2g

Fish Sandwich

Servings: 4
Cooking Time: 22 Minutes
Ingredients:
- 4 small cod fillets, skinless
- Salt and black pepper, to taste
- 2 tablespoons flour
- ¼ cup dried breadcrumbs
- Spray oil
- 9 ounces of frozen peas
- 1 tablespoon creme fraiche
- 12 capers
- 1 squeeze of lemon juice
- 4 bread rolls, cut in halve

Directions:
1. First, coat the cod fillets with flour, salt, and black pepper.
2. Then coat the fish with breadcrumbs.
3. Divide the coated codfish in the two crisper plates and spray them with cooking spray.
4. Return the crisper plate to the Tefal Dual Zone Air Fryer.
5. Choose the Air Fry mode for Zone 1 and set the temperature to 390 degrees F and the time to 17 minutes|
6. Select the "MATCH" button to copy the settings for Zone 2.
7. Initiate cooking by pressing the START/STOP button.
8. Meanwhile, boil peas in hot water for 5 minutes until soft.
9. Then drain the peas and transfer them to the blender.
10. Add capers, lemon juice, and crème fraiche to the blender.
11. Blend until it makes a smooth mixture.
12. Spread the peas crème mixture on top of 2 lower halves of the bread roll, and place the fish fillets on it.
13. Place the remaining bread slices on top.
14. Serve fresh.

Brown Sugar Garlic Salmon

Servings: 4
Cooking Time: 10 Minutes
Ingredients:
- 455g salmon
- Salt and black pepper, to taste
- 2 tablespoons brown sugar
- 1 teaspoon chili powder
- ½ teaspoon paprika
- 1 teaspoon Italian seasoning
- 1 teaspoon garlic powder

Directions:
1. Mix brown sugar with garlic powder, Italian seasoning, paprika, and chili powder in a bowl.
2. Rub this mixture over the salmon along with black pepper and salt.
3. Place the salmon in the air fryer baskets.
4. Return the air fryer basket 1 to Zone 1, and basket 2 to Zone 2 of the Tefal 2-Basket Air Fryer.
5. Choose the "Air Fry" mode for Zone 1 and set the temperature to 400 degrees F and 10 minutes of cooking time.
6. Select the "MATCH COOK" option to copy the settings for Zone 2.
7. Initiate cooking by pressing the START/PAUSE BUTTON.
8. Flip the salmon once cooked halfway through.
9. Serve warm.

Nutrition:
- (Per serving) Calories 275 | Fat 1.4g |Sodium 582mg | Carbs 31.5g | Fiber 1.1g | Sugar 0.1g | Protein 29.8g

Crispy Catfish

Servings: 4
Cooking Time: 17 Minutes
Ingredients:
- 4 catfish fillets
- ¼ cup Louisiana Fish fry
- 1 tablespoon olive oil
- 1 tablespoon parsley, chopped
- 1 lemon, sliced
- Fresh herbs, to garnish

Directions:
1. Mix fish fry with olive oil, and parsley then liberally rub over the catfish.
2. Place two fillets in each of the crisper plate.
3. Return the crisper plates to the Tefal Dual Zone Air Fryer.
4. Choose the Air Fry mode for Zone 1 and set the temperature to 390 degrees F and the time to 17 minutes|
5. Select the "MATCH" button to copy the settings for Zone 2.
6. Initiate cooking by pressing the START/STOP button.
7. Garnish with lemon slices and herbs.
8. Serve warm.

Salmon Nuggets

Servings: 4
Cooking Time: 15 Minutes
Ingredients:
- ⅓ cup maple syrup
- ¼ teaspoon dried chipotle pepper
- 1 pinch sea salt
- 1 ½ cups croutons
- 1 large egg
- 1 (1 pound) skinless salmon fillet, cut into 1 ½-inch chunk
- cooking spray

Directions:
1. Mix chipotle powder, maple syrup, and salt in a saucepan and cook on a simmer for 5 minutes|
2. Crush the croutons in a food processor and transfer to a bowl.
3. Beat egg in another shallow bowl.
4. Season the salmon chunks with sea salt.
5. Dip the salmon in the egg, then coat with breadcrumbs.
6. Divide the coated salmon chunks in the two crisper plates.
7. Return the crisper plate to the Tefal Dual Zone Air Fryer.
8. Select the Air Fry mode for Zone 1 and set the temperature to 390 degrees F and the time to 10 minutes|
9. Press the "MATCH" button to copy the settings for Zone 2.
10. Initiate cooking by pressing the START/STOP button.
11. Flip the chunks once cooked halfway through, then resume cooking.
12. Pour the maple syrup on top and serve warm.

Bang Bang Shrimp With Roasted Bok Choy

Servings: 4
Cooking Time: 13 Minutes

Ingredients:
- FOR THE BANG BANG SHRIMP
- ½ cup all-purpose flour
- 2 large eggs
- 1 cup panko bread crumbs
- 1 pound peeled shrimp (tails removed), thawed if frozen
- Nonstick cooking spray
- ½ cup mayonnaise
- ¼ cup Thai sweet chili sauce
- ¼ teaspoon sriracha
- FOR THE BOK CHOY
- 1 tablespoon reduced-sodium soy sauce
- 1 teaspoon minced garlic
- 1 teaspoon sesame oil
- 1 teaspoon minced fresh ginger
- 1½ pounds baby bok choy, halved lengthwise
- 1 tablespoon toasted sesame seeds

Directions:
1. To prep the shrimp: Set up a breading station with three small shallow bowls. Place the flour in the first bowl. In the second bowl, whisk the eggs. Place the panko in the third bowl.
2. Bread the shrimp in this order: First, dip them into the flour, coating both sides. Then, dip into the beaten egg. Finally, coat them in the panko, gently pressing the bread crumbs to adhere to the shrimp. Spritz both sides of the shrimp with cooking spray.
3. To prep the bok choy: In a small bowl, whisk together the soy sauce, garlic, sesame oil, and ginger.
4. To cook the shrimp and bok choy: Install a crisper plate in the Zone 1 basket. Place the shrimp in the basket in a single layer and insert the basket in the unit. Place the boy choy cut-side up in the Zone 2 basket. Pour the sauce over the bok choy and insert the basket in the unit.
5. Select Zone 1, select AIR FRY, set the temperature to 390°F, and set the timer to 13 minutes.
6. Select Zone 2, select BAKE, set the temperature to 370°F, and set the timer to 8 minutes. Select SMART FINISH.
7. Press START/PAUSE to begin cooking.
8. When cooking is complete, the shrimp should be cooked through and golden brown and the bok choy soft and slightly caramelized.
9. In a large bowl, whisk together the mayonnaise, sweet chili sauce, and sriracha. Add the shrimp and toss to coat.
10. Sprinkle the bok choy with the sesame seeds and serve hot alongside the shrimp.

Nutrition:
- (Per serving) Calories: 534; Total fat: 33g; Saturated fat: 4g; Carbohydrates: 29g; Fiber: 3g; Protein: 31g; Sodium: 789mg

Salmon With Broccoli And Cheese

Servings: 2
Cooking Time: 18

Ingredients:
- 2 cups of broccoli
- ½ cup of butter, melted
- Salt and pepper, to taste
- Oil spray, for greasing
- 1 cup of grated cheddar cheese
- 1 pound of salmon, fillets

Directions:
1. Take a bowl and add broccoli to it.
2. Add salt and black pepper and spray it with oil.
3. Put the broccoli in the air fryer zone 1 backset.
4. Now rub the salmon fillets with salt, black pepper, and butter.
5. Put it into zone 2 baskets.
6. Set zone 1 to air fry mode for 5 minters at 400 degrees F.
7. Set zone 2 to air fry mode for 18 minutes at 390 degrees F.
8. Hit start to start the cooking.
9. Once done, serve and by placing it on serving plates.
10. Put the grated cheese on top of the salmon and serve.

Nutrition:
- (Per serving) Calories 966 | Fat 79.1 g| Sodium 808 mg | Carbs 6.8 g | Fiber 2.4g | Sugar 1.9g | Protein 61.2 g

Chilean Sea Bass With Olive Relish And Snapper With Tomato

Servings: 4
Cooking Time: 15 Minutes

Ingredients:
- Chilean Sea Bass with Olive Relish:
- Olive oil spray
- 2 (170 g) Chilean sea bass fillets or other firm-fleshed white fish
- 3 tablespoons extra-virgin olive oil
- ½ teaspoon ground cumin
- ½ teaspoon kosher or coarse sea salt
- ½ teaspoon black pepper
- 60 g pitted green olives, diced
- 10 g finely diced onion
- 1 teaspoon chopped capers
- Snapper with Tomato:
- 2 snapper fillets
- 1 shallot, peeled and sliced
- 2 garlic cloves, halved
- 1 bell pepper, sliced
- 1 small-sized serrano pepper, sliced
- 1 tomato, sliced
- 1 tablespoon olive oil
- ¼ teaspoon freshly ground black pepper
- ½ teaspoon paprika
- Sea salt, to taste
- 2 bay leaves

Directions:
1. Make the Chilean Sea Bass with Olive Relish :
2. Spray the zone 1 air fryer drawer with the olive oil spray. Drizzle the fillets with the olive oil and sprinkle with the cumin, salt, and pepper. Place the fish in the zone 1 air fryer drawer. Set the air fryer to 164°C for 10 minutes, or until the fish flakes easily with a fork.
3. Meanwhile, in a small bowl, stir together the olives, onion, and capers.
4. Serve the fish topped with the relish.
5. Make the Snapper with Tomato :
6. Place two baking paper sheets on a working surface. Place the fish in the center of one side of the baking paper.
7. Top with the shallot, garlic, peppers, and tomato. Drizzle olive oil over the fish and vegetables. Season with black pepper, paprika, and salt. Add the bay leaves.
8. Fold over the other half of the baking paper. Now, fold the paper around the edges tightly and create a half moon shape, sealing the fish inside.
9. Cook in the zone 2 air fryer drawer at 200°C for 15 minutes. Serve warm.

Prawn Dejonghe Skewers

Servings: 4
Cooking Time: 15 Minutes

Ingredients:
- 2 teaspoons sherry, or apple cider vinegar
- 3 tablespoons unsalted butter, melted
- 120 g panko bread crumbs
- 3 cloves garlic, minced
- 8 g minced flat-leaf parsley, plus more for garnish
- 1 teaspoon kosher salt
- Pinch of cayenne pepper
- 680 g prawns, peeled and deveined
- Vegetable oil, for spraying
- Lemon wedges, for serving

Directions:
1. Stir the sherry and melted butter together in a shallow bowl or pie plate and whisk until combined. Set aside. Whisk together the panko, garlic, parsley, salt, and cayenne pepper on a large plate or shallow bowl.
2. Thread the prawns onto metal skewers designed for the air fryer or bamboo skewers, 3 to 4 per skewer. Dip 1 prawns skewer in the butter mixture, then dredge in the panko mixture until each prawns is lightly coated. Place the skewer on a plate or rimmed baking sheet and repeat the process with the remaining skewers.
3. Preheat the air fryer to 175°C. Arrange 4 skewers in the zone 1 air fryer basket. Spray the skewers with oil and air fry for 8 minutes, until the bread crumbs are golden brown and the prawns are cooked through. Transfer the cooked skewers to a serving plate and keep warm while cooking the remaining 4 skewers in the air fryer.
4. Sprinkle the cooked skewers with additional fresh parsley and serve with lemon wedges if desired.

Tuna Patty Sliders

Servings: 4
Cooking Time: 10 To 15 Minutes
Ingredients:
- 3 cans tuna, 140 g each, packed in water
- 40 g whole-wheat panko bread crumbs
- 50 g shredded Parmesan cheese
- 1 tablespoon Sriracha
- ¾ teaspoon black pepper
- 10 whole-wheat buns
- Cooking spray

Directions:
1. Preheat the air fryer to 175°C.
2. Spray the two air fryer baskets lightly with cooking spray.
3. In a medium bowl combine the tuna, bread crumbs, Parmesan cheese, Sriracha, and black pepper and stir to combine.
4. Form the mixture into 10 patties.
5. Place the patties in the two air fryer baskets in a single layer. Spray the patties lightly with cooking spray.
6. Air fry for 6 to 8 minutes. Turn the patties over and lightly spray with cooking spray. Air fry until golden brown and crisp, another 4 to 7 more minutes. Serve warm.

Tilapia With Mojo And Crispy Plantains

Servings: 4
Cooking Time: 30 Minutes
Ingredients:
- FOR THE TILAPIA
- 4 tilapia fillets (6 ounces each)
- 2 tablespoons all-purpose flour
- Nonstick cooking spray
- ¼ cup freshly squeezed orange juice
- 3 tablespoons fresh lime juice
- 2 tablespoons olive oil
- 1 tablespoon minced garlic
- ½ teaspoon ground cumin
- ¼ teaspoon kosher salt
- FOR THE PLANTAINS
- 1 large green plantain
- 2 cups cold water
- 2 teaspoons kosher salt
- Nonstick cooking spray

Directions:
1. To prep the tilapia: Dust both sides of the tilapia fillets with the flour, then spritz with cooking spray.
2. In a small bowl, whisk together the orange juice, lime juice, oil, garlic, cumin, and salt. Set the mojo sauce aside.
3. To prep the plantains: Cut the ends from the plantain, then remove and discard the peel. Slice the plantain into 1-inch rounds.
4. In a large bowl, combine the water, salt, and plantains. Let soak for 15 minutes.
5. Drain the plantains and pat them dry with paper towels. Spray with cooking spray.
6. To cook the tilapia and plantains: Install a crisper plate in each of the two baskets. Place the tilapia in a single layer in the Zone 1 basket (work in batches if needed) and insert the basket in the unit. Place the plantains in the Zone 2 basket and insert the basket in the unit.
7. Select Zone 1, select AIR FRY, set the temperature to 390°F, and set the timer to 10 minutes.
8. Select Zone 2, select AIR FRY, set the temperature to 390°F, and set the timer to 30 minutes. Select SMART FINISH.
9. Press START/PAUSE to begin cooking.
10. When the Zone 2 timer reads 10 minutes, press START/PAUSE. Remove the basket and use silicone-tipped tongs to transfer the plantains, which should be tender, to a cutting board. Use the bottom of a heavy glass to smash each plantain flat. Spray both sides with cooking spray and place them back in the basket. Reinsert the basket and press START/PAUSE to resume cooking.
11. When the Zone 1 timer reads 5 minutes, press START/PAUSE. Remove the basket. Spoon half of the mojo sauce over the tilapia. Reinsert the basket and press START/PAUSE to resume cooking.
12. When cooking is complete, the fish should be cooked through and the plantains crispy. Serve the tilapia and plantains with the remaining mojo sauce for dipping.

Nutrition:
- (Per serving) Calories: 380; Total fat: 21g; Saturated fat: 2g; Carbohydrates: 20g; Fiber: 1g; Protein: 35g; Sodium: 217mg

Pecan-crusted Catfish Nuggets With "fried" Okra

Servings: 4
Cooking Time: 17 Minutes

Ingredients:
- FOR THE CATFISH NUGGETS
- 1 cup whole milk
- 1 pound fresh catfish nuggets (or cut-up fillets)
- 1 large egg
- 2 to 3 dashes Louisiana-style hot sauce (optional)
- ¼ cup finely chopped pecans
- ½ cup all-purpose flour
- Nonstick cooking spray
- Tartar sauce, for serving (optional)
- FOR THE OKRA
- ½ cup fine yellow cornmeal
- ¼ cup all-purpose flour
- ½ teaspoon garlic powder
- ½ teaspoon paprika
- 1 teaspoon kosher salt
- 1 large egg
- 8 ounces frozen cut okra, thawed
- Nonstick cooking spray

Directions:
1. To prep the catfish: Pour the milk into a large zip-top bag. Add the catfish and turn to coat. Set in the refrigerator to soak for at least 1 hour or up to overnight.
2. Remove the fish from the milk, shaking off any excess liquid.
3. In a shallow dish, whisk together the egg and hot sauce (if using). In a second shallow dish, combine the pecans and flour.
4. Dip each piece of fish into the egg mixture, then into the nut mixture to coat. Gently press the nut mixture to adhere to the fish. Spritz each nugget with cooking spray.
5. To prep the okra: Set up a breading station with two small shallow bowls. In the first bowl, stir together the cornmeal, flour, garlic powder, paprika, and salt. In the second bowl, whisk the egg.
6. Dip the okra first in the cornmeal mixture, then the egg, then back into the cornmeal. Spritz with cooking spray.
7. To cook the catfish and okra: Install a crisper plate in each of the two baskets. Place the fish in a single layer in the Zone 1 basket and insert the basket in the unit. Place the okra in the Zone 2 basket and insert the basket in the unit.
8. Select Zone 1, select AIR FRY, set the temperature to 390°F, and set the timer to 17 minutes.
9. Select Zone 2, select AIR FRY, set the temperature to 400°F, and set the timer to 12 minutes. Select SMART FINISH.
10. Press START/PAUSE to begin cooking.
11. When cooking is complete, the fish should be cooked through and the okra golden brown and crispy. Serve hot.

Nutrition:
- (Per serving) Calories: 414; Total fat: 24g; Saturated fat: 2.5g; Carbohydrates: 30g; Fiber: 3g; Protein: 23g; Sodium: 569mg

Fried Tilapia

Servings: 4
Cooking Time: 20 Minutes

Ingredients:
- 4 fresh tilapia fillets, approximately 6 ounces each
- 2 teaspoons olive oil
- 2 teaspoons chopped fresh chives
- 2 teaspoons chopped fresh parsley
- 1 teaspoon minced garlic
- Freshly ground pepper, to taste
- Salt to taste

Directions:
1. Pat the tilapia fillets dry with a paper towel.
2. Stir together the olive oil, chives, parsley, garlic, salt, and pepper in a small bowl.
3. Brush the mixture over the top of the tilapia fillets.
4. Place a crisper plate in each drawer. Add the fillets in a single layer to each drawer. Insert the drawers into the unit.
5. Select zone 1, then AIR FRY, then set the temperature to 360 degrees F/ 180 degrees C with a 20-minute timer. To match zone 2 settings to zone 1, choose MATCH. To begin, select START/STOP.
6. Remove the tilapia fillets from the drawers after the timer has finished.

Nutrition:
- (Per serving) Calories 140 | Fat 5.7g | Sodium 125mg | Carbs 1.5g | Fiber 0.4g | Sugar 0g | Protein 21.7g

Seafood Shrimp Omelet

Servings: 2
Cooking Time: 15
Ingredients:
- 6 large shrimp, shells removed and chopped
- 6 eggs, beaten
- ½ tablespoon of butter, melted
- 2 tablespoons green onions, sliced
- 1/3 cup of mushrooms, chopped
- 1 pinch paprika
- Salt and black pepper, to taste
- Oil spray, for greasing

Directions:
1. In a large bowl whisk the eggs and add chopped shrimp, butter, green onions, mushrooms, paprika, salt, and black pepper.
2. Take two cake pans that fit inside the air fryer and grease them with oil spray.
3. Pour the egg mixture between the cake pans and place it in two baskets of the air fryer.
4. Turn on the BAKE function of zone 1, and let it cook for 15 minutes at 320 degrees F.
5. Select the MATCH button to match the cooking time for the zone 2 basket.
6. Once the cooking cycle completes, take out, and serve hot.

Nutrition:
- (Per serving) Calories 300 | Fat 17.5g| Sodium 368mg | Carbs 2.9g | Fiber 0.3g | Sugar1.4 g | Protein32.2 g

Honey Teriyaki Tilapia

Servings: 4
Cooking Time: 10 Minutes
Ingredients:
- 8 tablespoons low-sodium teriyaki sauce
- 3 tablespoons honey
- 2 garlic cloves, minced
- 2 tablespoons extra virgin olive oil
- 3 pieces tilapia (each cut into 2 pieces)

Directions:
1. Combine all the first 4 ingredients to make the marinade.
2. Pour the marinade over the tilapia and let it sit for 20 minutes.
3. Place a crisper plate in each drawer. Place the tilapia in the drawers. Insert the drawers into the unit.
4. Select zone 1, then AIR FRY, then set the temperature to 360 degrees F/ 180 degrees C with a 10-minute timer. To match zone 2 settings to zone 1, choose MATCH. To begin, select START/STOP.
5. Remove the tilapia from the drawers after the timer has finished.

Nutrition:
- (Per serving) Calories 350 | Fat 16.4g | Sodium 706mg | Carbs 19.3g | Fiber 0.1g | Sugar 19g | Protein 29.3g

Butter-wine Baked Salmon

Servings: 4
Cooking Time: 10 Minutes
Ingredients:
- 4 tablespoons butter, melted
- 2 cloves garlic, minced
- Sea salt and ground black pepper, to taste
- 60 ml dry white wine or apple cider vinegar
- 1 tablespoon lime juice
- 1 teaspoon smoked paprika
- ½ teaspoon onion powder
- 4 salmon steaks
- Cooking spray

Directions:
1. Place all the ingredients except the salmon and oil in a shallow dish and stir to mix well.
2. Add the salmon steaks, turning to coat well on both sides. Transfer the salmon to the refrigerator to marinate for 30 minutes.
3. Preheat the air fryer to 182ºC.
4. Place the salmon steaks in the two air fryer drawers, discarding any excess marinade. Spray the salmon steaks with cooking spray.
5. Air fry for about 10 minutes, flipping the salmon steaks halfway through, or until cooked to your preferred doneness.
6. Divide the salmon steaks among four plates and serve.

Garlic Butter Prawns Scampi & Coconut Prawns

Servings: 6
Cooking Time: 8 Minutes
Ingredients:
- Garlic Butter Prawns Scampi:
- Sauce:
- 60 g unsalted butter
- 2 tablespoons fish stock or chicken broth
- 2 cloves garlic, minced
- 2 tablespoons chopped fresh basil leaves
- 1 tablespoon lemon juice
- 1 tablespoon chopped fresh parsley, plus more for garnish
- 1 teaspoon red pepper flakes
- Prawns:
- 455 g large prawns, peeled and deveined, tails removed
- Fresh basil sprigs, for garnish
- Coconut Prawns:
- 230 g medium prawns, peeled and deveined
- 2 tablespoons salted butter, melted
- ½ teaspoon Old Bay seasoning
- 25 g desiccated, unsweetened coconut

Directions:
1. Make the Garlic Butter Prawns Scampi :
2. Preheat the air fryer to 175°C.
3. Put all the ingredients for the sauce in a baking pan and stir to incorporate.
4. Transfer the baking pan to the zone 1 air fryer basket and air fry for 3 minutes, or until the sauce is heated through.
5. Once done, add the prawns to the baking pan, flipping to coat in the sauce.
6. Return to the air fryer and cook for another 5 minutes, or until the prawns are pink and opaque. Stir the prawns twice during cooking.
7. Serve garnished with the parsley and basil sprigs.
8. Make the Coconut Prawns :
9. In a large bowl, toss the prawns in butter and Old Bay seasoning.
10. Place shredded coconut in bowl. Coat each piece of prawns in the coconut and place into the zone 2 air fryer basket.
11. Adjust the temperature to 205°C and air fry for 6 minutes.
12. Gently turn the prawns halfway through the cooking time. Serve immediately.

Simple Buttery Cod & Salmon On Bed Of Fennel And Carrot

Servings: 4
Cooking Time: 13 To 14 Minutes
Ingredients:
- Simple Buttery Cod:
- 2 cod fillets, 110 g each
- 2 tablespoons salted butter, melted
- 1 teaspoon Old Bay seasoning
- ½ medium lemon, sliced
- Salmon on Bed of Fennel and Carrot:
- 1 fennel bulb, thinly sliced
- 1 large carrot, peeled and sliced
- 1 small onion, thinly sliced
- 60 ml low-fat sour cream
- ¼ teaspoon coarsely ground pepper
- 2 salmon fillets, 140 g each

Directions:
1. Make the Simple Buttery Cod :
2. Place cod fillets into a round baking dish. Brush each fillet with butter and sprinkle with Old Bay seasoning. Lay two lemon slices on each fillet. Cover the dish with foil and place into the zone 1 air fryer basket.
3. Adjust the temperature to 175°C and bake for 8 minutes. Flip halfway through the cooking time. When cooked, internal temperature should be at least 65°C. Serve warm.
4. Make the Salmon on Bed of Fennel and Carrot :
5. Combine the fennel, carrot, and onion in a bowl and toss.
6. Put the vegetable mixture into a baking pan. Roast in the zone 2 air fryer basket at 205°C for 4 minutes or until the vegetables are crisp-tender.
7. Remove the pan from the air fryer. Stir in the sour cream and sprinkle the vegetables with the pepper.
8. Top with the salmon fillets.
9. Return the pan to the air fryer. Roast for another 9 to 10 minutes or until the salmon just barely flakes when tested with a fork.

Spicy Fish Fillet With Onion Rings

Servings: 1
Cooking Time: 12

Ingredients:
- 300 grams of onion rings, frozen and packed
- 1 codfish fillet, 8 ounces
- Salt and black pepper, to taste
- 1 teaspoon of lemon juice
- oil spray, for greasing

Directions:
1. Put the frozen onion rings in zone 1 basket of the air fryer.
2. Next pat dry the fish fillets with a paper towel and season them with salt, black pepper, and lemon juice.
3. Grease the fillet with oil spray.
4. Put the fish in zone 2 basket.
5. Use MAX crisp for zone 1 at 240 degrees for 9 minutes.
6. Use MAX crisp for zone 2 basket and set it to 210 degrees for 12 minutes.
7. Press sync and press start.
8. Once done, serve hot.

Nutrition:
- (Per serving) Calories 666| Fat23.5g| Sodium 911mg | Carbs 82g | Fiber 8.8g | Sugar 17.4g | Protein 30.4g

Lemon Pepper Fish Fillets

Servings: 4
Cooking Time: 10 Minutes

Ingredients:
- 4 tilapia fillets
- 30ml olive oil
- 2 tbsp lemon zest
- 1/8 tsp paprika
- 1 tsp garlic, minced
- 1 1/2 tsp ground peppercorns
- Pepper
- Salt

Directions:
1. In a small bowl, mix oil, peppercorns, paprika, garlic, lemon zest, pepper, and salt.
2. Brush the fish fillets with oil mixture.
3. Insert a crisper plate in the Tefal air fryer baskets.
4. Place fish fillets in both baskets.
5. Select zone 1 then select "air fry" mode and set the temperature to 390 degrees F for 10 minutes. Press "match" to match zone 2 settings to zone 1. Press "start/stop" to begin.

Nutrition:
- (Per serving) Calories 203 | Fat 9g |Sodium 99mg | Carbs 0.9g | Fiber 0.2g | Sugar 0.2g | Protein 32.1g

Classic Fish Sticks With Tartar Sauce

Servings: 4
Cooking Time: 12 To 15 Minutes

Ingredients:
- 680 g cod fillets, cut into 1-inch strips
- 1 teaspoon salt
- ½ teaspoon freshly ground black pepper
- 2 eggs
- 70 g almond flour
- 20 g grated Parmesan cheese
- Tartar Sauce:
- 120 ml sour cream
- 120 ml mayonnaise
- 3 tablespoons chopped dill pickle
- 2 tablespoons capers, drained and chopped
- ½ teaspoon dried dill
- 1 tablespoon dill pickle liquid (optional)

Directions:
1. Preheat the air fryer to 204°C. 2. Season the cod with the salt and black pepper; set aside. 3. In a shallow bowl, lightly beat the eggs. In a second shallow bowl, combine the almond flour and Parmesan cheese. Stir until thoroughly combined. 4. Working with a few pieces at a time, dip the fish into the egg mixture followed by the flour mixture. Press lightly to ensure an even coating. 5. Arrange the fish in a single layer in the two air fryer drawers and spray lightly with olive oil. Pausing halfway through the cooking time to turn the fish, air fry for 12 to 15 minutes, until the fish flakes easily with a fork. Let sit in the drawer for a few minutes before serving with the tartar sauce. 6. To make the tartar sauce: In a small bowl, combine the sour cream, mayonnaise, pickle, capers, and dill. If you prefer a thinner sauce, stir in the pickle liquid.

Cajun Catfish Cakes With Cheese

Servings: 4
Cooking Time: 35 Minutes
Ingredients:
- 2 catfish fillets
- 85 g butter
- 150 g shredded Parmesan cheese
- 150 g shredded Swiss cheese
- 120 ml buttermilk
- 1 teaspoon baking powder
- 1 teaspoon baking soda
- 1 teaspoon Cajun seasoning

Directions:
1. Bring a pot of salted water to a boil. Add the catfish fillets to the boiling water and let them boil for 5 minutes until they become opaque.
2. Remove the fillets from the pot to a mixing bowl and flake them into small pieces with a fork.
3. Add the remaining ingredients to the bowl of fish and stir until well incorporated.
4. Divide the fish mixture into 12 equal portions and shape each portion into a patty.
5. Preheat the air fryer to 190ºC.
6. Arrange the patties in the two air fryer baskets and air fry for 15 minutes until golden brown and cooked through. Flip the patties halfway through the cooking time.
7. Let the patties sit for 5 minutes and serve.

Breaded Scallops

Servings: 4
Cooking Time: 12 Minutes
Ingredients:
- ½ cup crushed buttery crackers
- ½ teaspoon garlic powder
- ½ teaspoon seafood seasoning
- 2 tablespoons butter, melted
- 1 pound sea scallops patted dry
- cooking spray

Directions:
1. Mix cracker crumbs, garlic powder, and seafood seasoning in a shallow bowl. Spread melted butter in another shallow bowl.
2. Dip each scallop in the melted butter and then roll in the breading to coat well.
3. Grease each Air fryer basket with cooking spray and place half of the scallops in each.
4. Return the crisper plate to the Tefal Dual Zone Air Fryer.
5. Select the Air Fry mode for Zone 1 and set the temperature to 390 degrees F and the time to 12 minutes|
6. Press the "MATCH" button to copy the settings for Zone 2.
7. Initiate cooking by pressing the START/STOP button.
8. Flip the scallops with a spatula after 4 minutes and resume cooking.
9. Serve warm.

Honey Pecan Shrimp

Servings: 4
Cooking Time: 10 Minutes
Ingredients:
- ¼ cup cornstarch
- ¾ teaspoon salt
- ¼ teaspoon black pepper
- 2 egg whites
- ⅔ cup pecans, chopped
- 455g shrimp, peeled, and deveined
- ¼ cup honey
- 2 tablespoons mayonnaise

Directions:
1. Mix cornstarch with ½ teaspoon black pepper, and ½ teaspoon salt in a bowl.
2. Mix pecans and ¼ teaspoon salt in another bowl.
3. Beat egg whites in another bowl.
4. Dredge the shrimp through the cornstarch mixture then dip in the egg whites.
5. Coat the shrimp with pecans mixture.
6. Divide the coated shrimp in the air fryer baskets.
7. Return the air fryer basket 1 to Zone 1, and basket 2 to Zone 2 of the Tefal 2-Basket Air Fryer.
8. Choose the "Air Fry" mode for Zone 1 at 330 degrees F and 10 minutes of cooking time.
9. Select the "MATCH COOK" option to copy the settings for Zone 2.
10. Initiate cooking by pressing the START/PAUSE BUTTON.
11. Flip the shrimps once cooked halfway through.
12. Serve.

Nutrition:
- (Per serving) Calories 155 | Fat 4.2g |Sodium 963mg | Carbs 21.5g | Fiber 0.8g | Sugar 5.7g | Protein 8.1g

Codfish With Herb Vinaigrette

Servings: 2
Cooking Time: 16
Ingredients:
- Vinaigrette Ingredients:
- 1/2 cup parsley leaves
- 1 cup basil leaves
- ½ cup mint leaves
- 2 tablespoons thyme leaves
- 1/4 teaspoon red pepper flakes
- 2 cloves of garlic
- 4 tablespoons of red wine vinegar
- ¼ cup of olive oil
- Salt, to taste
- Other Ingredients:
- 1.5 pounds fish fillets, cod fish
- 2 tablespoons olive oil
- Salt and black pepper, to taste
- 1 teaspoon of paprika
- 1teasbpoon of Italian seasoning

Directions:
1. Blend the entire vinaigrette ingredient in a high-speed blender and pulse into a smooth paste.
2. Set aside for drizzling overcooked fish.
3. Rub the fillets with salt, black pepper, paprika, Italian seasoning, and olive oil.
4. Divide it between two baskets of the air fryer.
5. Set the zone 1 to 16 minutes at 390 degrees F, at AIR FRY mode.
6. Press the MATCH button for the second basket.
7. Once done, serve the fillets with the drizzle of blended vinaigrette

Nutrition:
- (Per serving) Calories 1219| Fat 81.8g| Sodium 1906mg | Carbs64.4 g | Fiber5.5 g | Sugar 0.4g | Protein 52.1g

Blackened Mahimahi With Honey-roasted Carrots

Servings: 4
Cooking Time: 30 Minutes
Ingredients:
- FOR THE MAHIMAHI
- 4 mahimahi fillets (4 ounces each)
- 1 tablespoon olive oil
- 1 tablespoon blackening seasoning
- Lemon wedges, for serving
- FOR THE CARROTS
- 1 pound carrots, peeled and cut into ½-inch rounds
- 2 teaspoons vegetable oil
- ½ teaspoon kosher salt
- ¼ teaspoon freshly ground black pepper
- 1 tablespoon salted butter, cut into small pieces
- 1 tablespoon honey
- 2 tablespoons chopped fresh parsley

Directions:
1. To prep the mahimahi: Brush both sides of the fish with the oil and sprinkle with the blackening seasoning.
2. To prep the carrots: In a large bowl, combine the carrots, oil, salt, and black pepper. Stir well to coat the carrots with the oil.
3. To cook the mahimahi and carrots: Install a crisper plate in each of the two baskets. Place the fish in the Zone 1 basket and insert the basket in the unit. Place the carrots in the Zone 2 basket and insert the basket in the unit.
4. Select Zone 1, select AIR FRY, set the temperature to 380°F, and set the timer to 14 minutes.
5. Select Zone 2, select ROAST, set the temperature to 400°F, and set the timer to 30 minutes. Select SMART FINISH.
6. Press START/PAUSE to begin cooking.
7. When the Zone 2 timer reads 15 minutes, press START/PAUSE. Remove the basket and scatter the butter over the carrots, then drizzle them with the honey. Reinsert the basket and press START/PAUSE to resume cooking.
8. When cooking is complete, the fish should be cooked through and the carrots soft.
9. Stir the parsley into the carrots. Serve the fish with lemon wedges.

Nutrition:
- (Per serving) Calories: 235; Total fat: 9.5g; Saturated fat: 3g; Carbohydrates: 15g; Fiber: 3g; Protein: 22g; Sodium: 672mg

Cajun Scallops

Servings: 6
Cooking Time: 6 Minutes
Ingredients:
- 6 sea scallops
- Cooking spray
- Salt to taste
- Cajun seasoning

Directions:
1. Season the scallops with Cajun seasoning and salt.
2. Place them in one air fryer basket and spray them with cooking oil.
3. Return the air fryer basket 1 to Zone 1 of the Tefal 2-Basket Air Fryer.
4. Choose the "Air Fry" mode for Zone 1 and set the temperature to 400 degrees F and 6 minutes of cooking time.
5. Initiate cooking by pressing the START/PAUSE BUTTON.
6. Flip the scallops once cooked halfway through.
7. Serve warm.

Nutrition:
- (Per serving) Calories 266 | Fat 6.3g | Sodium 193mg | Carbs 39.1g | Fiber 7.2g | Sugar 5.2g | Protein 14.8g

Thai Prawn Skewers And Lemon-tarragon Fish En Papillote

Servings: 5
Cooking Time: 15 Minutes
Ingredients:
- Lemon-Tarragon Fish en Papillote:
- Salt and pepper, to taste
- 340 g extra-large prawns, peeled and deveined
- 1 tablespoon vegetable oil
- 1 teaspoon honey
- ½ teaspoon grated lime zest plus 1 tablespoon juice, plus lime wedges for serving
- 6 (6-inch) wooden skewers
- 3 tablespoons creamy peanut butter
- 3 tablespoons hot tap water
- 1 tablespoon chopped fresh coriander
- 1 teaspoon fish sauce
- Lemon-Tarragon Fish en Papillote:
- 2 tablespoons salted butter, melted
- 1 tablespoon fresh lemon juice
- ½ teaspoon dried tarragon, crushed, or 2 sprigs fresh tarragon
- 1 teaspoon kosher or coarse sea salt
- 85 g julienned carrots
- 435 g julienned fennel, or 1 stalk julienned celery
- 75 g thinly sliced red bell pepper
- 2 cod fillets, 170 g each, thawed if frozen
- Vegetable oil spray
- ½ teaspoon black pepper

Directions:
1. Make the Lemon-Tarragon Fish en Papillote :
2. Preheat the air fryer to 204°C.
3. Dissolve 2 tablespoons salt in 1 litre cold water in a large container. Add prawns, cover, and refrigerate for 15 minutes.
4. Remove prawns from brine and pat dry with paper towels. Whisk oil, honey, lime zest, and ¼ teaspoon pepper together in a large bowl. Add prawns and toss to coat. Thread prawns onto skewers, leaving about ¼ inch between each prawns .
5. Arrange 3 skewers in the zone 1 air fryer drawer, parallel to each other and spaced evenly apart. Arrange remaining 3 skewers on top, perpendicular to the bottom layer. Air fry until prawns are opaque throughout, 6 to 8 minutes, flipping and rotating skewers halfway through cooking.
6. Whisk peanut butter, hot tap water, lime juice, coriander, and fish sauce together in a bowl until smooth. Serve skewers with peanut dipping sauce and lime wedges.
7. Make the Lemon-Tarragon Fish en Papillote :
8. In a medium bowl, combine the butter, lemon juice, tarragon, and ½ teaspoon of the salt. Whisk well until you get a creamy sauce. Add the carrots, fennel, and bell pepper and toss to combine; set aside.
9. Cut two squares of baking paper each large enough to hold one fillet and half the vegetables. Spray the fillets with vegetable oil spray. Season both sides with the remaining ½ teaspoon salt and the black pepper.
10. Lay one fillet down on each baking paper square. Top each with half the vegetables. Pour any remaining sauce over the vegetables.
11. Fold over the baking paper and crimp the sides in small, tight folds to hold the fish, vegetables, and sauce securely inside the packet. Place the packets in the zone 2 air fryer drawer. Set the air fryer to 176°C for 15 minutes.
12. Transfer each packet to a plate. Cut open with scissors just before serving .

Glazed Scallops

Servings: 6
Cooking Time: 13 Minutes
Ingredients:
- 12 scallops
- 3 tablespoons olive oil
- Black pepper and salt to taste

Directions:
1. Rub the scallops with olive oil, black pepper, and salt.
2. Divide the scallops in the two crisper plates.
3. Return the crisper plate to the Tefal Dual Zone Air Fryer.
4. Choose the Air Fry mode for Zone 1 and set the temperature to 390 degrees F and the time to 13 minutes|
5. Select the "MATCH" button to copy the settings for Zone 2.
6. Initiate cooking by pressing the START/STOP button.
7. Flip the scallops once cooked halfway through, and resume cooking.
8. Serve warm.

Tender Juicy Honey Glazed Salmon

Servings: 4
Cooking Time:10 Minutes
Ingredients:
- 4 salmon fillets
- 1 tbsp honey
- 1/2 tsp red chili flakes, crushed
- 1 tsp sesame seeds, toasted
- 1 1/2 tsp olive oil
- 1 tbsp coconut aminos
- Pepper
- Salt

Directions:
1. Place salmon fillets into the bowl. In a small bowl, mix coconut aminos, oil, pepper, and salt and pour over fish fillets. Mix well.
2. Cover bowl and place in the refrigerator for 20 minutes.
3. Preheat the air fryer to 400 F.
4. Place marinated salmon fillets into the air fryer basket and cook for 8 minutes.
5. Brush fish fillets with honey and sprinkle with chili flakes and sesame seeds and cook for 2 minutes more.
6. Serve and enjoy.

Two-way Salmon

Servings:2
Cooking Time:18
Ingredients:
- 2 salmon fillets, 8 ounces each
- 2 tablespoons of Cajun seasoning
- 2 tablespoons of jerk seasoning
- 1 lemon cut in half
- oil spray, for greasing

Directions:
1. First, drizzle lemon juice over the salmon and wash it with tap water.
2. Rinse and pat dry the fillets with a paper towel.
3. Now rub o fillet with Cajun seasoning and grease it with oil spray.
4. Take the second fillet and rub it with jerk seasoning.
5. Grease the second fillet of salmon with oil spray.
6. now put the salmon fillets in both the baskets.
7. Set the Zone 1 basket to 390 degrees F for 16-18 minutes
8. Select MATCH button for zone 2 basket.
9. hit the start button to start cooking.
10. Once the cooking is done, serve the fish hot with mayonnaise.

Nutrition:
- (Per serving) Calories 238| Fat 11.8g| Sodium 488mg | Carbs 9g | Fiber 0g | Sugar8 g | Protein 35g

Poultry Recipes

Chicken Thighs With Coriander

Servings: 4
Cooking Time: 25 Minutes
Ingredients:
- 1 tablespoon olive oil
- Juice of ½ lime
- 1 tablespoon coconut aminos
- 1½ teaspoons Montreal chicken seasoning
- 8 bone-in chicken thighs, skin on
- 2 tablespoons chopped fresh coriander

Directions:
1. In a gallon-size resealable bag, combine the olive oil, lime juice, coconut aminos, and chicken seasoning. Add the chicken thighs, seal the bag, and massage the bag to ensure the chicken is thoroughly coated. Refrigerate for at least 2 hours, preferably overnight.
2. Preheat the air fryer to 200°C.
3. Remove the chicken from the marinade and arrange in a single layer in the two air fryer baskets. Pausing halfway through the cooking time to flip the chicken, air fry for 20 to 25 minutes, until a thermometer inserted into the thickest part registers 75°C.
4. Transfer the chicken to a serving platter and top with the coriander before serving.

Turkey Burger Patties

Servings: 4
Cooking Time: 14 Minutes
Ingredients:
- 1 egg white
- 453g ground turkey
- 30ml Worcestershire sauce
- ½ tsp dried basil
- ½ tsp dried oregano
- Pepper
- Salt

Directions:
1. In a bowl, mix ground turkey with remaining ingredients until well combined.
2. Insert a crisper plate in the Tefal air fryer baskets.
3. Make patties from the turkey mixture and place them in both baskets.
4. Select zone 1, then select "air fry" mode and set the temperature to 360 degrees F for 14 minutes. Press "match" to match zone 2 settings to zone 1. Press "start/stop" to begin.

Nutrition:
- (Per serving) Calories 234 | Fat 12.5g | Sodium 251mg | Carbs 1.7g | Fiber 0.1g | Sugar 1.6g | Protein 32g

Buffalo Chicken

Servings: 4
Cooking Time: 22 Minutes
Ingredients:
- ½ cup plain fat-free Greek yogurt
- ¼ cup egg substitute
- 1 tablespoon plus 1 teaspoon hot sauce
- 1 cup panko breadcrumbs
- 1 tablespoon sweet paprika
- 1 tablespoon garlic pepper seasoning
- 1 tablespoon cayenne pepper
- 1-pound skinless, boneless chicken breasts, cut into 1-inch strips

Directions:
1. Combine the Greek yogurt, egg substitute, and hot sauce in a mixing bowl.
2. In a separate bowl, combine the panko breadcrumbs, paprika, garlic powder, and cayenne pepper.
3. Dip the chicken strips in the yogurt mixture, then coat them in the breadcrumb mixture.
4. Install a crisper plate in both drawers. Place the chicken strips into the drawers and then insert the drawers into the unit.
5. Select zone 1, select AIR FRY, set temperature to 390 degrees F/ 200 degrees C, and set time to 22 minutes. Select MATCH to match zone 2 settings to zone 1. Press the START/STOP button to begin cooking.
6. When cooking is complete, serve immediately.

Nutrition:
- (Per serving) Calories 234 | Fat 15.8g | Sodium 696mg | Carbs 22.1g | Fiber 1.1g | Sugar 1.7g | Protein 31.2g

Cracked-pepper Chicken Wings

Servings: 4
Cooking Time: 20 Minutes
Ingredients:
- 450 g chicken wings
- 3 tablespoons vegetable oil
- 60 g all-purpose flour
- ½ teaspoon smoked paprika
- ½ teaspoon garlic powder
- ½ teaspoon kosher salt
- 1½ teaspoons freshly cracked black pepper

Directions:
1. Place the chicken wings in a large bowl. Drizzle the vegetable oil over wings and toss to coat.
2. In a separate bowl, whisk together the flour, paprika, garlic powder, salt, and pepper until combined.
3. Dredge the wings in the flour mixture one at a time, coating them well, and place in the zone 1 air fryer drawer. Set the temperature to 200°C for 20 minutes, turning the wings halfway through the cooking time, until the breading is browned and crunchy.

Sweet-and-sour Chicken With Pineapple Cauliflower Rice

Servings: 4
Cooking Time: 30 Minutes
Ingredients:
- FOR THE CHICKEN
- ¼ cup cornstarch, plus 2 teaspoons
- ¼ teaspoon kosher salt
- 2 large eggs
- 1 tablespoon sesame oil
- 1½ pounds boneless, skinless chicken breasts, cut into 1-inch pieces
- Nonstick cooking spray
- 6 tablespoons ketchup
- ¾ cup apple cider vinegar
- 1½ tablespoons soy sauce
- 1 tablespoon sugar
- FOR THE CAULIFLOWER RICE
- 1 cup finely diced fresh pineapple
- 1 red bell pepper, thinly sliced
- 1 small red onion, thinly sliced
- 1 tablespoon vegetable oil
- 2 cups frozen cauliflower rice, thawed
- 2 tablespoons soy sauce
- 1 teaspoon sesame oil
- 2 scallions, sliced

Directions:
1. To prep the chicken:
2. Set up a breading station with two small shallow bowls. Combine ¼ cup of cornstarch and the salt in the first bowl. In the second bowl, beat the eggs with the sesame oil.
3. Dip the chicken pieces in the cornstarch mixture to coat, then into the egg mixture, then back into the cornstarch mixture to coat. Mist the coated pieces with cooking spray.
4. In a small bowl, whisk together the ketchup, vinegar, soy sauce, sugar, and remaining 2 teaspoons of cornstarch.
5. To prep the cauliflower rice: Blot the pineapple dry with a paper towel. In a large bowl, combine the pineapple, bell pepper, onion, and vegetable oil.
6. To cook the chicken and cauliflower rice: Install a crisper plate in each of the two baskets. Place the chicken in the Zone 1 basket and insert the basket in the unit. Place a piece of aluminum foil over the crisper plate in the Zone 2 basket and add the pineapple mixture. Insert the basket in the unit.
7. Select Zone 1, select AIR FRY, set the temperature to 400°F, and set the time to 30 minutes.
8. Select Zone 2, select AIR BROIL, set the temperature to 450°F, and set the time to 12 minutes. Select SMART FINISH.
9. Press START/PAUSE to begin cooking.
10. When the Zone 2 timer reads 4 minutes, press START/PAUSE. Remove the basket and stir in the cauliflower rice, soy sauce, and sesame oil. Reinsert the basket and press START/PAUSE to resume cooking.
11. When cooking is complete, the chicken will be golden brown and cooked through and the rice warmed through. Stir the scallions into the rice and serve.

Chipotle Drumsticks

Servings: 4
Cooking Time: 20 Minutes
Ingredients:
- 1 tablespoon tomato paste
- ½ teaspoon chipotle powder
- ¼ teaspoon apple cider vinegar
- ¼ teaspoon garlic powder
- 8 chicken drumsticks
- ½ teaspoon salt
- ⅛ teaspoon ground black pepper

Directions:
1. In a small bowl, combine tomato paste, chipotle powder, vinegar, and garlic powder.
2. Sprinkle drumsticks with salt and pepper, then place into a large bowl and pour in tomato paste mixture. Toss or stir to evenly coat all drumsticks in mixture.
3. Place drumsticks into two ungreased air fryer baskets. Adjust the temperature to 200°C and air fry for 25 minutes, turning drumsticks halfway through cooking. Drumsticks will be dark red with an internal temperature of at least 75°C when done. Serve warm.

Marinated Chicken Legs

Servings: 6
Cooking Time: 28 Minutes
Ingredients:
- 6 chicken legs
- 15ml olive oil
- 1 tsp ground mustard
- 36g brown sugar
- ¼ tsp cayenne
- 1 tsp smoked paprika
- 1 tsp garlic powder
- 1 tsp onion powder
- Pepper
- Salt

Directions:
1. Add the chicken legs and the remaining ingredients into a zip-lock bag. Seal the bag and place in the refrigerator for 4 hours.
2. Insert a crisper plate in the Tefal air fryer baskets.
3. Place the marinated chicken legs in both baskets.
4. Select zone 1, then select "bake" mode and set the temperature to 390 degrees F for 25-28 minutes. Press "match" to match zone 2 settings to zone 1. Press "start/stop" to begin.

Nutrition:
- (Per serving) Calories 308 | Fat 17.9g | Sodium 128mg | Carbs 5.5g | Fiber 0.3g | Sugar 4.7g | Protein 29.9g

Chicken Strips With Satay Sauce

Servings: 4
Cooking Time: 10 Minutes
Ingredients:
- 4 (170 g) boneless, skinless chicken breasts, sliced into 16 (1-inch) strips
- 1 teaspoon fine sea salt
- 1 teaspoon paprika
- Sauce:
- 60 g creamy almond butter (or sunflower seed butter for nut-free)
- 2 tablespoons chicken broth
- 1½ tablespoons coconut vinegar or unseasoned rice vinegar
- 1 clove garlic, minced
- 1 teaspoon peeled and minced fresh ginger
- ½ teaspoon hot sauce
- ⅛ teaspoon stevia glycerite, or 2 to 3 drops liquid stevia
- For Garnish/Serving (Optional):
- 15 g chopped coriander leaves
- Red pepper flakes
- Sea salt flakes
- Thinly sliced red, orange, and yellow bell peppers
- Special Equipment:
- 16 wooden or bamboo skewers, soaked in water for 15 minutes

Directions:
1. Spray the zone 1 air fryer drawer with avocado oil. Preheat the air fryer to 200°C. 2. Thread the chicken strips onto the skewers. Season on all sides with the salt and paprika. Place the chicken skewers in the air fryer drawer and air fry for 5 minutes, flip, and cook for another 5 minutes, until the chicken is cooked through and the internal temperature reaches 76°C. 3. While the chicken skewers cook, make the sauce: In a medium-sized bowl, stir together all the sauce ingredients until well combined. Taste and adjust the sweetness and heat to your liking. 4. Garnish the chicken with coriander, red pepper flakes, and salt flakes, if desired, and serve with sliced bell peppers, if desired. Serve the sauce on the side. 5. Store leftovers in an airtight container in the fridge for up to 4 days or in the freezer for up to a month. Reheat in a preheated 180°C air fryer for 3 minutes per side, or until heated through.

Garlic Dill Wings

Servings: 4
Cooking Time: 25 Minutes
Ingredients:
- 900 g bone-in chicken wings, separated at joints
- ½ teaspoon salt
- ½ teaspoon ground black pepper
- ½ teaspoon onion powder
- ½ teaspoon garlic powder
- 1 teaspoon dried dill

Directions:
1. In a large bowl, toss wings with salt, pepper, onion powder, garlic powder, and dill until evenly coated. Place wings into the two ungreased air fryer drawers in a single layer.
2. Adjust the temperature to 200°C and air fry for 25 minutes, shaking the drawer every 7 minutes during cooking. Wings should have an internal temperature of at least 76°C and be golden brown when done. Serve warm.

Curried Orange Honey Chicken

Servings: 4
Cooking Time: 16 To 19 Minutes
Ingredients:
- 340 g boneless, skinless chicken thighs, cut into 1-inch pieces
- 1 yellow bell pepper, cut into 1½-inch pieces
- 1 small red onion, sliced
- Olive oil for misting
- 60 ml chicken stock
- 2 tablespoons honey
- 60 ml orange juice
- 1 tablespoon cornflour
- 2 to 3 teaspoons curry powder

Directions:
1. Preheat the air fryer to 190°C.
2. Put the chicken thighs, pepper, and red onion in the zone 1 air fryer drawer and mist with olive oil.
3. Roast for 12 to 14 minutes or until the chicken is cooked to 76°C, shaking the drawer halfway through cooking time.
4. Remove the chicken and vegetables from the air fryer drawer and set aside.
5. In a metal bowl, combine the stock, honey, orange juice, cornflour, and curry powder, and mix well. Add the chicken and vegetables, stir, and put the bowl in the drawer.
6. Return the drawer to the air fryer and roast for 2 minutes. Remove and stir, then roast for 2 to 3 minutes or until the sauce is thickened and bubbly.
7. Serve warm.

Thai Chicken Meatballs

Servings: 4
Cooking Time: 10 Minutes
Ingredients:
- ½ cup sweet chili sauce
- 2 tablespoons lime juice
- 2 tablespoons ketchup
- 1 teaspoon soy sauce
- 1 large egg, lightly beaten
- ¾ cup panko breadcrumbs
- 1 green onion, finely chopped
- 1 tablespoon minced fresh cilantro
- ½ teaspoon salt
- ½ teaspoon garlic powder
- 1-pound lean ground chicken

Directions:
1. Combine the chili sauce, lime juice, ketchup, and soy sauce in a small bowl; set aside ½ cup for serving.
2. Combine the egg, breadcrumbs, green onion, cilantro, salt, garlic powder, and the remaining 4 tablespoons chili sauce mixture in a large mixing bowl. Mix in the chicken lightly yet thoroughly. Form into 12 balls.
3. Install a crisper plate in both drawers. Place half the chicken meatballs in the zone 1 drawer and half in zone 2's, then insert the drawers into the unit.
4. Select zone 1, select AIR FRY, set temperature to 390 degrees F/ 200 degrees C, and set time to 10 minutes. Select MATCH to match zone 2 settings to zone 1. Press the START/STOP button to begin cooking.
5. When the time reaches 5 minutes, press START/STOP to pause the unit. Remove the drawers and flip the chicken. Re-insert the drawers into the unit and press START/STOP to resume cooking.
6. When cooking is complete, remove the chicken meatballs and serve hot.

Nutrition:
- (Per serving) Calories 93 | Fat 3g | Sodium 369mg | Carbs 9g | Fiber 0g | Sugar 6g | Protein 9g

Spice-rubbed Chicken Pieces

Servings: 6
Cooking Time: 40
Ingredients:
- 3 pounds chicken, pieces
- 1 teaspoon sweet paprika
- 1 teaspoon mustard powder
- 1 tablespoon brown sugar, dark
- Salt and black pepper, to taste
- 1 teaspoon Chile powder, New Mexico
- 1 teaspoon oregano, dried
- ¼ teaspoon allspice powder, ground

Directions:
1. Take a bowl and mix dark brown sugar, salt, paprika, mustard powder, oregano, Chile powder, black pepper, and all spice powder.
2. Mix well and rub this spice mixture all over the chicken.
3. Divide the chicken between two air fryer baskets.
4. Oil sprays the meat and then adds it to the air fryer.
5. Now press button1 and button 2 and set the time to 40 minutes at 350 degrees F.
6. Now press start and once the cooking cycle completes, press pause for both the zones.
7. Take out the chicken and serve hot.

Nutrition:
- (Per serving) Calories 353 | Fat 7.1g | Sodium 400 mg | Carbs 2.2g | Fiber 0.4 g | Sugar 1.6g | Protein 66 g

Simply Terrific Turkey Meatballs

Servings: 4
Cooking Time: 7 To 10 Minutes
Ingredients:
- 1 red bell pepper, seeded and coarsely chopped
- 2 cloves garlic, coarsely chopped
- 15 g chopped fresh parsley
- 680 g 85% lean turkey mince
- 1 egg, lightly beaten
- 45 g grated Parmesan cheese
- 1 teaspoon salt
- ½ teaspoon freshly ground black pepper

Directions:
1. Preheat the air fryer to 200°C.
2. In a food processor fitted with a metal blade, combine the bell pepper, garlic, and parsley. Pulse until finely chopped. Transfer the vegetables to a large mixing bowl.
3. Add the turkey, egg, Parmesan, salt, and black pepper. Mix gently until thoroughly combined. Shape the mixture into 1¼-inch meatballs.
4. Arrange the meatballs in a single layer in the two air fryer drawers; coat lightly with olive oil spray. Pausing halfway through the cooking time to shake the drawer, air fry for 7 to 10 minutes, until lightly browned and a thermometer inserted into the centre of a meatball registers 76°C.

Lemon Chicken Thighs

Servings: 4
Cooking Time: 25 Minutes
Ingredients:
- ¼ cup butter, softened
- 3 garlic cloves, minced
- 2 teaspoons minced fresh rosemary or ½ teaspoon crushed dried rosemary
- 1 teaspoon minced fresh thyme or ¼ teaspoon dried thyme
- 1 teaspoon grated lemon zest
- 1 tablespoon lemon juice
- 4 bone-in chicken thighs (about 1½ pounds)
- 1/8 teaspoon salt
- 1/8 teaspoon pepper

Directions:
1. Combine the butter, garlic, rosemary, thyme, lemon zest, and lemon juice in a small bowl.
2. Under the skin of each chicken thigh, spread 1 teaspoon of the butter mixture. Apply the remaining butter to each thigh's skin. Season to taste with salt and pepper.
3. Install a crisper plate in both drawers. Place half the chicken tenders in the zone 1 drawer and half in zone 2's, then insert the drawers into the unit.
4. Select zone 1, select AIR FRY, set temperature to 390 degrees F/ 200 degrees C, and set time to 22 minutes. Select MATCH to match zone 2 settings to zone 1. Press the START/STOP button to begin cooking.
5. When the time reaches 11 minutes, press START/STOP to pause the unit. Remove the drawers and flip the chicken. Re-insert the drawers into the unit and press START/STOP to resume cooking.
6. When cooking is complete, remove the chicken and serve.

Nutrition:
- (Per serving) Calories 329 | Fat 26g | Sodium 253mg | Carbs 1g | Fiber 0g | Sugar 0g | Protein 23g

Roasted Garlic Chicken Pizza With Cauliflower "wings"

Servings: 4
Cooking Time: 25 Minutes
Ingredients:
- FOR THE PIZZA
- 2 prebaked rectangular pizza crusts or flatbreads
- 2 tablespoons olive oil
- 1 tablespoon minced garlic
- 1½ cups shredded part-skim mozzarella cheese
- 6 ounces boneless, skinless chicken breast, thinly sliced
- ¼ teaspoon red pepper flakes (optional)
- FOR THE CAULIFLOWER "WINGS"
- 4 cups cauliflower florets
- 1 tablespoon vegetable oil
- ½ cup Buffalo wing sauce

Directions:
1. To prep the pizza:
2. Trim the pizza crusts to fit in the air fryer basket, if necessary.
3. Brush the top of each crust with the oil and sprinkle with the garlic. Top the crusts with the mozzarella, chicken, and red pepper flakes .
4. To prep the cauliflower "wings": In a large bowl, combine the cauliflower and oil and toss to coat the florets.
5. To cook the pizza and "wings":
6. Install a crisper plate in each of the two baskets. Place one pizza in the Zone 1 basket and insert the basket in the unit. Place the cauliflower in the Zone 2 basket and insert the basket in the unit.
7. Select Zone 1, select ROAST, set the temperature to 375°F, and set the time to 25 minutes.
8. Select Zone 2, select AIR FRY, set the temperature to 390°F, and set the time to 25 minutes. Select SMART FINISH.
9. Press START/PAUSE to begin cooking.
10. When the Zone 1 timer reads 13 minutes, press START/PAUSE. Remove the basket. Transfer the pizza to a cutting board . Add the second pizza to the basket. Reinsert the basket in the unit and press START/PAUSE to resume cooking.
11. When the Zone 2 timer reads 5 minutes, press START/PAUSE. Remove the basket and add the Buffalo wing sauce to the cauliflower. Shake well to evenly coat the cauliflower in the sauce. Reinsert the basket and press START/PAUSE to resume cooking.
12. When cooking is complete, the cauliflower will be crisp on the outside and tender inside, and the chicken on the second pizza will be cooked through and the cheese melted.
13. Cut each pizza into 4 slices. Serve with the cauliflower "wings" on the side.

Brazilian Chicken Drumsticks

Servings: 6
Cooking Time: 47 Minutes
Ingredients:
- 2 teaspoons cumin seeds
- 2 teaspoons dried parsley
- 2 teaspoons turmeric powder
- 2 teaspoons dried oregano leaves
- 2 teaspoons salt
- 1 teaspoon coriander seeds
- 1 teaspoon black peppercorns
- 1 teaspoon cayenne pepper
- ½ cup lime juice
- 4 tablespoons vegetable oil
- 3 lbs. chicken drumsticks

Directions:
1. Grind cumin, parsley, salt, coriander seeds, cayenne pepper, peppercorns, oregano, and turmeric in a food processor.
2. Add this mixture to lemon juice and oil in a bowl and mix well.
3. Rub the spice paste over the chicken drumsticks and let them marinate for 30 minutes|
4. Divide the chicken drumsticks in both the crisper plates.
5. Return the crisper plates to the Tefal Dual Zone Air Fryer.
6. Choose the Air Fry mode for Zone 1 and set the temperature to 390 degrees F and the time to 47 minutes|
7. Select the "MATCH" button to copy the settings for Zone 2.
8. Initiate cooking by pressing the START/STOP button.
9. Flip the drumsticks when cooked halfway through, then resume cooking.
10. Serve warm.

Juicy Paprika Chicken Breast

Servings: 4
Cooking Time: 30 Minutes
Ingredients:
- Oil, for spraying
- 4 (170 g) boneless, skinless chicken breasts
- 1 tablespoon olive oil
- 1 tablespoon paprika
- 1 tablespoon packed light brown sugar
- ½ teaspoon cayenne pepper
- ½ teaspoon onion powder
- ½ teaspoon granulated garlic

Directions:
1. Line the two air fryer drawers with parchment and spray lightly with oil.
2. Brush the chicken with the olive oil.
3. In a small bowl, mix together the paprika, brown sugar, cayenne pepper, onion powder, and garlic and sprinkle it over the chicken.
4. Place the chicken in the two prepared drawers.
5. Air fry at 180°C for 15 minutes, flip, and cook for another 15 minutes, or until the internal temperature reaches 76°C. Serve immediately.

Wild Rice And Kale Stuffed Chicken Thighs

Servings: 4
Cooking Time: 22 Minutes
Ingredients:
- 4 boneless, skinless chicken thighs
- 250 g cooked wild rice
- 35 g chopped kale
- 2 garlic cloves, minced
- 1 teaspoon salt
- Juice of 1 lemon
- 100 g crumbled feta
- Olive oil cooking spray
- 1 tablespoon olive oi

Directions:
1. Preheat the air fryer to 192°C.
2. Place the chicken thighs between two pieces of plastic wrap, and using a meat mallet or a rolling pin, pound them out to about ¼-inch thick.
3. In a medium bowl, combine the rice, kale, garlic, salt, and lemon juice and mix well.
4. Place a quarter of the rice mixture into the middle of each chicken thigh, then sprinkle 2 tablespoons of feta over the filling.
5. Spray the two air fryer drawers with olive oil cooking spray.
6. Fold the sides of the chicken thigh over the filling, and then gently place each of them seam-side down into the two air fryer drawers. Brush each stuffed chicken thigh with olive oil.
7. Roast the stuffed chicken thighs for 12 minutes, then turn them over and cook for an additional 10 minutes, or until the internal temperature reaches 76°C.

Buttermilk Fried Chicken

Servings: 6
Cooking Time: 30 Minutes
Ingredients:
- 1½ pounds boneless, skinless chicken thighs
- 2 cups buttermilk
- 1 cup all-purpose flour
- 1 tablespoon seasoned salt
- ½ tablespoon ground black pepper
- 1 cup panko breadcrumbs
- Cooking spray

Directions:
1. Place the chicken thighs in a shallow baking dish. Cover with the buttermilk. Refrigerate for 4 hours or overnight.
2. In a large gallon-sized resealable bag, combine the flour, seasoned salt, and pepper.
3. Remove the chicken from the buttermilk but don't discard the mixture.
4. Add the chicken to the bag and shake well to coat.
5. Dip the thighs in the buttermilk again, then coat in the panko breadcrumbs.
6. Install a crisper plate in each drawer. Place half the chicken thighs in the zone 1 drawer and half in zone 2's, then insert the drawers into the unit.
7. Select zone 1, select AIR FRY, set temperature to 390 degrees F/ 200 degrees C, and set time to 30 minutes. Select MATCH to match zone 2 settings to zone 1. Press the START/STOP button to begin cooking.
8. When the time reaches 15 minutes, press START/STOP to pause the unit. Remove the drawers and flip the chicken. Re-insert the drawers into the unit and press START/STOP to resume cooking.
9. When cooking is complete, remove the chicken.

Nutrition:
- (Per serving) Calories 335 | Fat 12.8g | Sodium 687mg | Carbs 33.1g | Fiber 0.4g | Sugar 4g | Protein 24.5g

General Tso's Chicken

Servings: 4
Cooking Time: 22 Minutes
Ingredients:
- 1 egg, large
- ⅓ cup 2 teaspoons cornstarch,
- ¼ teaspoons salt
- ¼ teaspoons ground white pepper
- 7 tablespoons chicken broth
- 2 tablespoons soy sauce
- 2 tablespoons ketchup
- 2 teaspoons sugar
- 2 teaspoons unseasoned rice vinegar
- 1 ½ tablespoons canola oil
- 4 chile de árbol, chopped and seeds discarded
- 1 tablespoon chopped fresh ginger
- 1 tablespoon garlic, chopped
- 2 tablespoons green onion, sliced
- 1 teaspoon toasted sesame oil
- 1 lb. boneless chicken thighs, cut into 1 ¼ -inch chunks
- ½ teaspoon toasted sesame seeds

Directions:
1. Add egg to a large bowl and beat it with a fork.
2. Add chicken to the egg and coat it well.
3. Whisk ⅓ cup of cornstarch with black pepper and salt in a small bowl.
4. Add chicken to the cornstarch mixture and mix well to coat.
5. Divide the chicken in the two crisper plates and spray them cooking oi.
6. Return the crisper plates to the Tefal Dual Zone Air Fryer.
7. Choose the Air Fry mode for Zone 1 and set the temperature to 390 degrees F and the time to 20 minutes|
8. Select the "MATCH" button to copy the settings for Zone 2.
9. Initiate cooking by pressing the START/STOP button.
10. Once done, remove the air fried chicken from the air fryer.
11. Whisk 2 teaspoons of cornstarch with soy sauce, broth, sugar, ketchup, and rice vinegar in a small bowl.
12. Add chilies and canola oil to a skillet and sauté for 1 minute.
13. Add garlic and ginger, then sauté for 30 seconds.
14. Stir in cornstarch sauce and cook until it bubbles and thickens.
15. Toss in cooked chicken and garnish with sesame oil, sesame seeds, and green onion.
16. Enjoy.

Sweet And Spicy Carrots With Chicken Thighs

Servings:2
Cooking Time:35
Ingredients:
- Cooking spray, for greasing
- 2 tablespoons butter, melted
- 1 tablespoon hot honey
- 1 teaspoon orange zest
- 1 teaspoon cardamom
- ½ pound baby carrots
- 1 tablespoon orange juice
- Salt and black pepper, to taste
- ½ pound of carrots, baby carrots
- 8 chicken thighs

Directions:
1. Take a bowl and mix all the glaze ingredients in it.
2. Now, coat the chicken and carrots with the glaze and let it rest for 30 minutes.
3. Now place the chicken thighs into the zone 1 basket.
4. Next put the glazed carrots into the zone 2 basket.
5. Press button 1 for the first basket and set it to ROAST Mode at 350 degrees F for 35 minutes.
6. For the second basket hit 2 and set time to AIRFRY mode at 390 degrees F for 8-10 minutes.
7. Once the cooking cycle completes take out the carrots and chicken and serve it hot.

Nutrition:
- (Per serving) Calories 1312| Fat 55.4g| Sodium 757mg | Carbs 23.3g | Fiber6.7 g | Sugar12 g | Protein171 g

Honey-glazed Chicken Thighs

Servings: 4
Cooking Time: 14 Minutes
Ingredients:
- Oil, for spraying
- 4 boneless, skinless chicken thighs, fat trimmed
- 3 tablespoons soy sauce
- 1 tablespoon balsamic vinegar
- 2 teaspoons honey
- 2 teaspoons minced garlic
- 1 teaspoon ground ginger

Directions:
1. Preheat the zone 1 air fryer drawer to 200°C. Line the zone 1 air fryer drawer with parchment and spray lightly with oil.
2. Place the chicken in the prepared drawer.
3. Cook for 7 minutes, flip, and cook for another 7 minutes, or until the internal temperature reaches 76°C and the juices run clear.
4. In a small saucepan, combine the soy sauce, balsamic vinegar, honey, garlic, and ginger and cook over low heat for 1 to 2 minutes, until warmed through.
5. Transfer the chicken to a serving plate and drizzle with the sauce just before serving.

Asian Chicken

Servings: 4
Cooking Time: 12 Minutes
Ingredients:
- 8 chicken thighs, boneless
- 4 garlic cloves, minced
- 85g honey
- 120ml soy sauce
- 1 tsp dried oregano
- 2 tbsp parsley, chopped
- 1 tbsp ketchup

Directions:
1. Add chicken and remaining ingredients in a bowl and mix until well coated. Cover and place in the refrigerator for 6 hours.
2. Insert a crisper plate in the Tefal air fryer baskets.
3. Remove the chicken from the marinade and place them in both baskets.
4. Select zone 1 then select "air fry" mode and set the temperature to 390 degrees F for 12 minutes. Press "match" to match zone 2 settings to zone 1. Press "start/stop" to begin.

Nutrition:
- (Per serving) Calories 646 | Fat 21.7g | Sodium 2092mg | Carbs 22.2g | Fiber 0.6g | Sugar 18.9g | Protein 86.9g

Teriyaki Chicken Skewers

Servings: 4
Cooking Time: 16 Minutes
Ingredients:
- 455g boneless chicken thighs, cubed
- 237ml teriyaki marinade
- 16 small wooden skewers
- Sesame seeds for rolling
- Teriyaki Marinade
- ⅓ cup soy sauce
- 59ml chicken broth
- ½ orange, juiced
- 2 tablespoons brown sugar
- 1 teaspoon ginger, grated
- 1 clove garlic, grated

Directions:
1. Blend teriyaki marinade ingredients in a blender.
2. Add chicken and its marinade to a Ziplock bag.
3. Seal this bag, shake it well and refrigerate for 30 minutes.
4. Thread the chicken on the wooden skewers.
5. Place these skewers in the air fryer baskets.
6. Return the air fryer basket 1 to Zone 1, and basket 2 to Zone 2 of the Tefal 2-Basket Air Fryer.
7. Choose the "Air Fry" mode for Zone 1 at 350 degrees F and 16 minutes of cooking time.
8. Select the "MATCH COOK" option to copy the settings for Zone 2.
9. Initiate cooking by pressing the START/PAUSE BUTTON.
10. Flip the skewers once cooked halfway through.
11. Garnish with sesame seeds.
12. Serve warm.

Nutrition:
- (Per serving) Calories 456 | Fat 16.4g | Sodium 1321mg | Carbs 19.2g | Fiber 2.2g | Sugar 4.2g | Protein 55.2g

Wings With Corn On The Cob

Servings: 2
Cooking Time: 40 Minutes
Ingredients:
- 6 chicken wings, skinless
- 2 tablespoons coconut amino
- 2 tablespoons brown sugar
- 1 teaspoon ginger, paste
- ½ inch garlic, minced
- Salt and black pepper to taste
- 2 corn on cobs, small
- Oil spray, for greasing

Directions:
1. Spray the corns with oil spray and season them with salt.
2. Coat the chicken wings with coconut amino, brown sugar, ginger, garlic, salt, and black pepper.
3. Spray the wings with a good amount of oil spray.
4. Put the chicken wings in the zone 1 basket.
5. Put the corn into the zone 2 basket.
6. Select ROAST mode for the chicken wings and set the time to 23 minutes at 400 degrees F/ 200 degrees C.
7. Press 2 and select the AIR FRY mode for the corn and set the time to 40 at 300 degrees F/ 150 degrees C.
8. Once it's done, serve and enjoy.

Nutrition:
- (Per serving) Calories 950 | Fat 33.4g | Sodium 592 mg | Carbs 27.4g | Fiber 2.1g | Sugar 11.3 g | Protein 129g

Apricot-glazed Turkey Tenderloin

Servings: 4
Cooking Time: 30 Minutes
Ingredients:
- Olive oil
- 80 g sugar-free apricot preserves
- ½ tablespoon spicy brown mustard
- 680 g turkey breast tenderloin
- Salt and freshly ground black pepper, to taste

Directions:
1. Spray the two air fryer drawers lightly with olive oil.
2. In a small bowl, combine the apricot preserves and mustard to make a paste.
3. Season the turkey with salt and pepper. Spread the apricot paste all over the turkey.
4. Place the turkey in the two air fryer drawers and lightly spray with olive oil.
5. Air fry at 190°C for 15 minutes. Flip the turkey over and lightly spray with olive oil. Air fry until the internal temperature reaches at least 80°C, an additional 10 to 15 minutes.
6. Let the turkey rest for 10 minutes before slicing and serving.

Chicken & Broccoli

Servings: 4
Cooking Time: 20 Minutes
Ingredients:
- 450g chicken breasts, boneless & cut into 1-inch pieces
- 1 tsp sesame oil
- 15ml soy sauce
- 1 tsp garlic powder
- 45ml olive oil
- 350g broccoli florets
- 2 tsp hot sauce
- 2 tsp rice vinegar
- Pepper
- Salt

Directions:
1. In a bowl, add chicken, broccoli florets, and remaining ingredients and mix well.
2. Insert a crisper plate in the Tefal air fryer baskets.
3. Add the chicken and broccoli mixture in both baskets.
4. Select zone 1, then select "air fry" mode and set the temperature to 380 degrees F for 20 minutes. Press "match" and press "start/stop" to begin.

Nutrition:
- (Per serving) Calories 337 | Fat 20.2g | Sodium 440mg | Carbs 3.9g | Fiber 1.3g | Sugar 1g | Protein 34.5g

Fajita Chicken Strips & Barbecued Chicken With Creamy Coleslaw

Servings: 6
Cooking Time: 20 Minutes
Ingredients:
- Fajita Chicken Strips:
- 450 g boneless, skinless chicken tenderloins, cut into strips
- 3 bell peppers, any color, cut into chunks
- 1 onion, cut into chunks
- 1 tablespoon olive oil
- 1 tablespoon fajita seasoning mix
- Cooking spray
- Barbecued Chicken with Creamy Coleslaw:
- 270 g shredded coleslaw mix
- Salt and pepper
- 2 (340 g) bone-in split chicken breasts, trimmed
- 1 teaspoon vegetable oil
- 2 tablespoons barbecue sauce, plus extra for serving
- 2 tablespoons mayonnaise
- 2 tablespoons sour cream
- 1 teaspoon distilled white vinegar, plus extra for seasoning
- ¼ teaspoon sugar

Directions:
1. Make the Fajita Chicken Strips :
2. Preheat the air fryer to 190°C.
3. In a large bowl, mix together the chicken, bell peppers, onion, olive oil, and fajita seasoning mix until completely coated.
4. Spray the zone 1 air fryer basket lightly with cooking spray.
5. Place the chicken and vegetables in the zone 1 air fryer basket and lightly spray with cooking spray.
6. Air fry for 7 minutes. Shake the basket and air fry for an additional 5 to 8 minutes, until the chicken is cooked through and the veggies are starting to char.
7. Serve warm.
8. Make the Barbecued Chicken with Creamy Coleslaw :
9. Preheat the air fryer to 180°C.
10. Toss coleslaw mix and ¼ teaspoon salt in a colander set over bowl. Let sit until wilted slightly, about 30 minutes. Rinse, drain, and dry well with a dish towel.
11. Meanwhile, pat chicken dry with paper towels, rub with oil, and season with salt and pepper. Arrange breasts skin-side down in zone 2 air fryer basket, spaced evenly apart, alternating ends. Bake for 10 minutes. Flip breasts and brush skin side with barbecue sauce. Return basket to air fryer and bake until well browned and chicken registers 70°C, 10 to 15 minutes.
12. Transfer chicken to serving platter, tent loosely with aluminum foil, and let rest for 5 minutes. While chicken rests, whisk mayonnaise, sour cream, vinegar, sugar, and pinch pepper together in a large bowl. Stir in coleslaw mix and season with salt, pepper, and additional vinegar to taste. Serve chicken with coleslaw, passing extra barbecue sauce separately.

Chicken Shawarma

Servings: 4
Cooking Time: 15 Minutes
Ingredients:
- Shawarma Spice:
- 2 teaspoons dried oregano
- 1 teaspoon ground cinnamon
- 1 teaspoon ground cumin
- 1 teaspoon ground coriander
- 1 teaspoon kosher salt
- ½ teaspoon ground allspice
- ½ teaspoon cayenne pepper
- Chicken:
- 450 g boneless, skinless chicken thighs, cut into large bite-size chunks
- 2 tablespoons vegetable oil
- For Serving:
- Tzatziki
- Pita bread

Directions:
1. For the shawarma spice: In a small bowl, combine the oregano, cayenne, cumin, coriander, salt, cinnamon, and allspice. 2. For the chicken: In a large bowl, toss together the chicken, vegetable oil, and shawarma spice to coat. Marinate at room temperature for 30 minutes or cover and refrigerate for up to 24 hours. 3. Place the chicken in the zone 1 air fryer basket. Set the air fryer to 180°C for 15 minutes, or until the chicken reaches an internal temperature of 75°C. 4. Transfer the chicken to a serving platter. Serve with tzatziki and pita bread.

Jamaican Fried Chicken

Servings: 6
Cooking Time: 25 Minutes
Ingredients:
- 6-8 chicken thighs
- Egg Marinade:
- 2 teaspoons of hot sauce
- 1 teaspoon of ground ginger
- 1 teaspoon of ground onion
- 1 teaspoon of black pepper
- 1 teaspoon of ground garlic
- 237ml of almond milk
- 1 tablespoon of lemon juice
- 1 large egg
- Breading:
- 2 cups of ground almonds
- ⅓ cup of tapioca starch
- 1 tablespoon of paprika
- 1 tablespoon of thyme
- 1 tablespoon of parsley
- 1 teaspoon of garlic powder
- 1 teaspoon of onion powder
- ½ teaspoon of cayenne pepper
- 1 teaspoon of pink salt
- Spray on cooking oil olive oil spray

Directions:
1. Mix egg marinade ingredients in a large bowl and add chicken thighs.
2. Stir well to coat then cover and refrigerate for 30 minutes.
3. Meanwhile, mix all the breading ingredients in a shallow bowl.
4. Remove the chicken from the egg marinade and coat with the breading mixture.
5. Place the coated chicken thighs in the air fryer baskets.
6. Return the air fryer basket 1 to Zone 1, and basket 2 to Zone 2 of the Tefal 2-Basket Air Fryer.
7. Choose the "Air Fry" mode for Zone 1 and set the temperature to 375 degrees F and 25 minutes of cooking time.
8. Select the "MATCH COOK" option to copy the settings for Zone 2.
9. Initiate cooking by pressing the START/PAUSE BUTTON.
10. Flip the chicken thighs once cooked halfway through.
11. Serve.

Nutrition:
- (Per serving) Calories 268 | Fat 10.4g | Sodium 411mg | Carbs 0.4g | Fiber 0.1g | Sugar 0.1g | Protein 40.6g

Crumbed Chicken Katsu

Servings: 4
Cooking Time: 26 Minutes
Ingredients:
- 1 lb. boneless chicken breast, cut in half
- 2 large eggs, beaten
- 1 ½ cups panko bread crumbs
- Salt and black pepper ground to taste
- Cooking spray
- Sauce:
- 1 tablespoon sugar
- 2 tablespoons soy sauce
- 1 tablespoon sherry
- ½ cup ketchup
- 2 teaspoons Worcestershire sauce
- 1 teaspoon garlic, minced

Directions:
1. Mix soy sauce, ketchup, sherry, sugar, garlic, and Worcestershire sauce in a mixing bowl.
2. Keep this katsu aside for a while.
3. Rub the chicken pieces with salt and black pepper.
4. Whisk eggs in a shallow dish and spread breadcrumbs in another tray.
5. Dip the chicken in the egg mixture and coat them with breadcrumbs.
6. Place the coated chicken in the two crisper plates and spray them with cooking spray.
7. Return the crisper plate to the Tefal Dual Zone Air Fryer.
8. Choose the Air Fry mode for Zone 1 and set the temperature to 390 degrees F and the time to 26 minutes|
9. Select the "MATCH" button to copy the settings for Zone 2.
10. Initiate cooking by pressing the START/STOP button.
11. Flip the chicken once cooked halfway through, then resume cooking.
12. Serve warm with the sauce.

Chicken Legs With Leeks

Servings: 6
Cooking Time: 18 Minutes
Ingredients:
- 2 leeks, sliced
- 2 large-sized tomatoes, chopped
- 3 cloves garlic, minced
- ½ teaspoon dried oregano
- 6 chicken legs, boneless and skinless
- ½ teaspoon smoked cayenne pepper
- 2 tablespoons olive oil
- A freshly ground nutmeg

Directions:
1. In a mixing dish, thoroughly combine all ingredients, minus the leeks. Place in the refrigerator and let it marinate overnight.
2. Lay the leeks onto the bottom of the two air fryer drawers. Top with the chicken legs.
3. Roast chicken legs at 190°C for 18 minutes, turning halfway through. Serve with hoisin sauce.

Yummy Chicken Breasts

Servings: 2
Cooking Time: 25
Ingredients:
- 4 large chicken breasts, 6 ounces each
- 2 tablespoons of oil bay seasoning
- 1 tablespoon Montreal chicken seasoning
- 1 teaspoon of thyme
- 1/2 teaspoon of paprika
- Salt, to taste
- oil spray, for greasing

Directions:
1. Season the chicken breast pieces with the listed seasoning and let them rest for 40 minutes.
2. Grease both sides of the chicken breast pieces with oil spray.
3. Divide the chicken breast piece between both baskets.
4. Set zone 1 to AIRFRY mode at 400 degrees F, for 15 minutes.
5. Select the MATCH button for another basket.
6. Select pause and take out the baskets and flip the chicken breast pieces, after 15 minutes.
7. Select the zones to 400 degrees F for 10 more minutes using the MATCH cook button.
8. Once it's done serve.

Nutrition:
- (Per serving) Calories 711| Fat 27.7g| Sodium 895mg | Carbs 1.6g | Fiber 0.4g | Sugar 0.1g | Protein 106.3g

Chicken Kebabs

Servings: 4
Cooking Time: 9 Minutes
Ingredients:
- 455g boneless chicken breast, cut into 1-inch pieces
- 1 tablespoon avocado oil
- 1 tablespoon Tamari soy sauce
- 1 teaspoon garlic powder
- 1 teaspoon ground ginger
- 1 teaspoon chili powder
- 1 tablespoon honey
- 1 green capsicum, cut into 1-inch pieces
- 1 red capsicum, cut into 1-inch pieces
- 1 yellow capsicum, cut into 1-inch pieces
- 1 courgette, cut into 1-inch pieces
- 1 small red onion, cut into 1-inch pieces
- cooking spray

Directions:
1. Rub chicken with oil and place in a bowl.
2. Mix honey, chili powder, ginger, garlic and soy sauce in a bowl.
3. Pour this mixture over the chicken.
4. Cover and marinate the chicken for 15 minutes.
5. Thread the marinated chicken with veggies on wooden skewers alternately.
6. Divide the skewers and place in the air fryer baskets.
7. Return the air fryer basket 1 to Zone 1, and basket 2 to Zone 2 of the Tefal 2-Basket Air Fryer.
8. Choose the "Air Fry" mode for Zone 1 at 350 degrees F and 9 minutes of cooking time.
9. Select the "MATCH COOK" option to copy the settings for Zone 2.
10. Initiate cooking by pressing the START/PAUSE BUTTON.
11. Flip the skewers once cooked halfway through.
12. Serve warm.

Nutrition:
- (Per serving) Calories 546 | Fat 33.1g |Sodium 1201mg | Carbs 30g | Fiber 2.4g | Sugar 9.7g | Protein 32g

Orange Chicken With Roasted Snap Peas And Scallions

Servings: 4
Cooking Time: 30 Minutes
Ingredients:
- FOR THE CHICKEN
- ⅓ cup all-purpose flour
- 2 large eggs
- ⅓ cup cornstarch, plus 2 tablespoons
- 1½ pounds boneless, skinless chicken breasts, cut into 1-inch pieces
- Nonstick cooking spray
- 2 tablespoons grated orange zest
- 1 cup freshly squeezed orange juice
- ¼ cup granulated sugar
- 2 tablespoons rice vinegar
- 2 tablespoons soy sauce
- ¼ teaspoon minced fresh ginger
- ¼ teaspoon grated garlic
- FOR THE SNAP PEAS
- 8 ounces snap peas
- 1 tablespoon vegetable oil
- ½ teaspoon minced garlic
- ½ teaspoon grated fresh ginger
- ¼ teaspoon kosher salt
- ¼ teaspoon freshly ground black pepper
- 4 scallions, thinly sliced

Directions:
1. To prep the chicken:
2. Set up a breading station with three small shallow bowls. Place the flour in the first bowl. In the second bowl, beat the eggs. Place ⅓ cup of cornstarch in the third bowl.
3. Bread the chicken pieces in this order: First, dip them into the flour to coat. Then, dip into the beaten egg. Finally, add them to the cornstarch, coating all sides. Mist the breaded chicken with cooking spray.
4. In a small bowl, whisk together the orange zest, orange juice, sugar, vinegar, soy sauce, ginger, garlic, and remaining 2 tablespoons of cornstarch. Set orange sauce aside.
5. To prep the snap peas: In a large bowl, combine the snap peas, oil, garlic, ginger, salt, and black pepper. Toss to coat.
6. To cook the chicken and snap peas: Install a crisper plate in the Zone 1 basket. Add the chicken to the basket and insert the basket in the unit. Place the snap peas in the Zone 2 basket and insert the basket in the unit.
7. Select Zone 1, select AIR FRY, set the temperature to 400°F, and set the time to 30 minutes.
8. Select Zone 2, select ROAST, set the temperature to 375°F, and set the time to 12 minutes. Select SMART FINISH.
9. Press START/PAUSE to begin cooking.
10. When the Zone 1 timer reads 15 minutes, press START/PAUSE. Remove the basket and shake to redistribute the chicken. Reinsert the basket and press START/PAUSE to resume cooking.
11. When the Zone 1 timer reads 5 minutes, press START/PAUSE. Remove the basket and pour the reserved orange sauce over the chicken. Reinsert the basket and press START/PAUSE to resume cooking.
12. When cooking is complete, the chicken and vegetables will be cooked through. Stir the scallions into the snap peas. Serve hot.

Chicken Vegetable Skewers

Servings: 6
Cooking Time: 15 Minutes
Ingredients:
- 900g chicken breasts, cubed
- 1 bell pepper, chopped
- 51g Swerve
- 1 tsp ginger, grated
- 350g zucchini, chopped
- 8 mushrooms, sliced
- ½ medium onion, chopped
- 6 garlic cloves, crushed
- 120ml soy sauce

Directions:
1. Add chicken and the remaining ingredients to a zip-lock bag. Seal the bag and place it in the refrigerator overnight.
2. Thread the marinated chicken, zucchini, mushrooms, onion, and bell pepper onto the skewers.
3. Insert a crisper plate in the Tefal air fryer baskets.
4. Place skewers in both baskets.
5. Select zone 1 then select "air fry" mode and set the temperature to 380 degrees F for 15 minutes. Press "match" to match zone 2 settings to zone 1. Press "start/stop" to begin.

Nutrition:
- (Per serving) Calories 329 | Fat 11.5g | Sodium 1335mg | Carbs 8.6g | Fiber 1.4g | Sugar 2.9g | Protein 46.8g

Goat Cheese–stuffed Chicken Breast With Broiled Zucchini And Cherry Tomatoes

Servings: 4
Cooking Time: 25 Minutes

Ingredients:
- FOR THE STUFFED CHICKEN BREASTS
- 2 ounces soft goat cheese
- 1 tablespoon minced fresh parsley
- ½ teaspoon minced garlic
- 4 boneless, skinless chicken breasts (6 ounces each)
- 1 tablespoon vegetable oil
- ½ teaspoon Italian seasoning
- ½ teaspoon kosher salt
- ½ teaspoon freshly ground black pepper
- FOR THE ZUCCHINI AND TOMATOES
- 1 pound zucchini, diced
- 1 cup cherry tomatoes, halved
- 1 tablespoon vegetable oil
- ½ teaspoon kosher salt
- ¼ teaspoon freshly ground black pepper

Directions:
1. To prep the stuffed chicken breasts:
2. In a small bowl, combine the goat cheese, parsley, and garlic. Mix well.
3. Cut a deep slit into the fatter side of each chicken breast to create a pocket . Stuff each breast with the goat cheese mixture. Use a toothpick to secure the opening of the chicken, if needed.
4. Brush the outside of the chicken breasts with the oil and season with the Italian seasoning, salt, and black pepper.
5. To prep the zucchini and tomatoes: In a large bowl, combine the zucchini, tomatoes, and oil. Mix to coat. Season with salt and black pepper.
6. To cook the chicken and vegetables:
7. Install a crisper plate in each of the two baskets. Insert a broil rack in the Zone 2 basket over the crisper plate. Place the chicken in the Zone 1 basket and insert the basket in the unit. Place the vegetables on the broiler rack in the Zone 2 basket and insert the basket in the unit.
8. Select Zone 1, select AIR FRY, set the temperature to 390°F, and set the time to 25 minutes.
9. Select Zone 2, select AIR BROIL, set the temperature to 450°F, and set the time to 10 minutes. Select SMART FINISH.
10. Press START/PAUSE to begin cooking.
11. When cooking is complete, the chicken will be golden brown and cooked through and the zucchini will be soft and slightly charred. Serve hot.

Crispy Sesame Chicken

Servings: 2
Cooking Time: 10 Minutes

Ingredients:
- 680g boneless chicken thighs, diced
- 2 tablespoons rice vinegar
- 1 tablespoon soy sauce
- 2 teaspoons minced fresh ginger
- 1 garlic clove, minced
- ¾ teaspoon salt
- ½ teaspoon black pepper
- 2 large eggs, beaten
- 1 cup cornstarch
- Sauce
- 59ml soy sauce
- 2 tablespoons rice vinegar
- ⅓ cup brown sugar
- 59ml water
- 1 tablespoon cornstarch
- 2 teaspoons sesame oil
- 2 tablespoons vegetable oil
- 2 garlic cloves, minced
- 2 teaspoons chile paste
- Garnish
- 1 tablespoon toasted sesame seeds

Directions:
1. Blend all the sauce ingredients in a saucepan and cook until it thickens then allow it to cool.
2. Mix chicken with black pepper, salt, garlic, ginger, vinegar, and soy sauce in a bowl.
3. Cover and marinate the chicken for 20 minutes.
4. Divide the chicken in the air fryer baskets.
5. Return the air fryer basket 1 to Zone 1, and basket 2 to Zone 2 of the Tefal 2-Basket Air Fryer.
6. Choose the "Air Fry" mode for Zone 1 and set the temperature to 400 degrees F and 10 minutes of cooking time.
7. Select the "MATCH COOK" option to copy the settings for Zone 2.
8. Initiate cooking by pressing the START/PAUSE BUTTON.
9. Pour the prepared sauce over the air fried chicken and drizzle sesame seeds on top.
10. Serve warm.

Nutrition:
- (Per serving) Calories 351 | Fat 16g |Sodium 777mg | Carbs 26g | Fiber 4g | Sugar 5g | Protein 28g

Bell Pepper Stuffed Chicken Roll-ups

Servings: 4
Cooking Time: 12 Minutes

Ingredients:
- 2 (115 g) boneless, skinless chicken breasts, slice in half horizontally
- 1 tablespoon olive oil
- Juice of ½ lime
- 2 tablespoons taco seasoning
- ½ green bell pepper, cut into strips
- ½ red bell pepper, cut into strips
- ¼ onion, sliced

Directions:
1. Preheat the air fryer to 200°C.
2. Unfold the chicken breast slices on a clean work surface. Rub with olive oil, then drizzle with lime juice and sprinkle with taco seasoning.
3. Top the chicken slices with equal amount of bell peppers and onion. Roll them up and secure with toothpicks.
4. Arrange the chicken roll-ups in the preheated air fryer. Air fry for 12 minutes or until the internal temperature of the chicken reaches at least 75°C. Flip the chicken roll-ups halfway through.
5. Remove the chicken from the air fryer. Discard the toothpicks and serve immediately.

Coconut Chicken Tenders With Broiled Utica Greens

Servings: 4
Cooking Time: 25 Minutes

Ingredients:
- FOR THE CHICKEN TENDERS
- 2 tablespoons all-purpose flour
- 2 large eggs
- 1 cup unsweetened shredded coconut
- ¾ cup panko bread crumbs
- ½ teaspoon kosher salt
- 1½ pounds chicken tenders
- Nonstick cooking spray
- FOR THE UTICA GREENS
- 12 ounces frozen chopped escarole or Swiss chard, thawed and drained
- ¼ cup diced prosciutto
- 2 tablespoons chopped pickled cherry peppers
- ½ teaspoon garlic powder
- ½ teaspoon onion powder
- ¼ teaspoon kosher salt
- ¼ cup Italian-style bread crumbs
- ¼ cup grated Romano cheese
- Nonstick cooking spray

Directions:
1. To prep the chicken tenders:
2. Set up a breading station with three small shallow bowls. Place the flour in the first bowl. In the second bowl, beat the eggs. Combine the coconut, bread crumbs, and salt in the third bowl.
3. Bread the chicken tenders in this order: First, coat them in the flour. Then, dip into the beaten egg. Finally, coat them in the coconut breading, gently pressing the breading into the chicken to help it adhere. Mist both sides of each tender with cooking spray.
4. To prep the Utica greens: In the Zone 2 basket, mix the greens, prosciutto, cherry peppers, garlic powder, onion powder, and salt. Scatter the bread crumbs and Romano cheese over the top. Spritz the greens with cooking spray.
5. To cook the chicken and greens:
6. Install a crisper plate in the Zone 1 basket. Place the chicken tenders in the basket in a single layer and insert the basket in the unit. Insert the Zone 2 basket in the unit.
7. Select Zone 1, select AIR FRY, set the temperature to 390°F, and set the time to 25 minutes.
8. Select Zone 2, select AIR BROIL, set the temperature to 450°F, and set the time to 10 minutes. Select SMART FINISH.
9. Press START/PAUSE to begin cooking.
10. When cooking is complete, the chicken will be crispy and cooked through and the greens should be warmed through and toasted on top. Serve warm.

Beef, Pork, And Lamb Recipes

Bacon Wrapped Pork Tenderloin

Servings: 2
Cooking Time: 20 Minutes
Ingredients:
- ½ teaspoon salt
- ¼ teaspoon black pepper
- 1 pork tenderloin
- 6 center cut strips bacon
- cooking string

Directions:
1. Cut two bacon strips in half and place them on the working surface.
2. Place the other bacon strips on top and lay the tenderloin over the bacon strip.
3. Wrap the bacon around the tenderloin and tie the roast with a kitchen string.
4. Place the roast in the first air fryer basket.
5. Return the air fryer basket 1 to Zone 1, and basket 2 to Zone 2 of the Tefal 2-Basket Air Fryer.
6. Choose the "Air Fry" mode for Zone 1 and set the temperature to 400 degrees F and 20 minutes of cooking time.
7. Initiate cooking by pressing the START/PAUSE BUTTON.
8. Slice and serve warm.

Easy Breaded Pork Chops

Servings: 8
Cooking Time: 20 Minutes
Ingredients:
- 1 egg
- 118ml milk
- 8 pork chops
- 1 packet ranch seasoning
- 238g breadcrumbs
- Pepper
- Salt

Directions:
1. In a small bowl, whisk the egg and milk.
2. In a separate shallow dish, mix breadcrumbs, ranch seasoning, pepper, and salt.
3. Dip each pork chop in the egg mixture, then coat with breadcrumbs.
4. Insert a crisper plate in the Tefal air fryer baskets.
5. Place the coated pork chops in both baskets.
6. Select zone 1, then select air fry mode and set the temperature to 360 degrees F for 12 minutes. Press "match" to match zone 2 settings to zone 1. Press "start/stop" to begin. Turn halfway through.

Kheema Burgers

Servings: 4
Cooking Time: 12 Minutes
Ingredients:
- Burgers:
- 450 g 85% lean beef mince or lamb mince
- 2 large eggs, lightly beaten
- 1 medium brown onion, diced
- 60 ml chopped fresh coriander
- 1 tablespoon minced fresh ginger
- 3 cloves garlic, minced
- 2 teaspoons garam masala
- 1 teaspoon ground turmeric
- ½ teaspoon ground cinnamon
- ⅛ teaspoon ground cardamom
- 1 teaspoon coarse or flaky salt
- 1 teaspoon cayenne pepper
- Raita Sauce:
- 235 ml grated cucumber
- 120 ml sour cream
- ¼ teaspoon coarse or flaky salt
- ¼ teaspoon black pepper
- For Serving:
- 4 lettuce leaves, hamburger buns, or naan breads

Directions:
1. For the burgers: In a large bowl, combine the beef mince, eggs, onion, coriander, ginger, garlic, garam masala, turmeric, cinnamon, cardamom, salt, and cayenne. Gently mix until ingredients are thoroughly combined. 2. Divide the meat into four portions and form into round patties. Make a slight depression in the middle of each patty with your thumb to prevent them from puffing up into a dome shape while cooking. 3. Place the patties in the zone 1 air fryer drawer. Set the temperature to 176°C for 12 minutes. Use a meat thermometer to ensure the burgers have reached an internal temperature of 72°C . 4. Meanwhile, for the sauce: In a small bowl, combine the cucumber, sour cream, salt, and pepper. 5. To serve: Place the burgers on the lettuce, buns, or naan and top with the sauce.

Strip Steaks With Hasselback Potatoes

Servings: 4
Cooking Time: 30 Minutes
Ingredients:
- FOR THE STRIP STEAK
- 2 boneless strip steaks (8 ounces each)
- 2 teaspoons vegetable oil
- 1 tablespoon steak seasoning
- FOR THE HASSELBACK POTATOES
- 4 russet potatoes
- 1 tablespoon vegetable oil
- 1 teaspoon kosher salt
- 1 tablespoon salted butter, at room temperature
- 2 teaspoons minced garlic
- 2 teaspoons minced fresh parsley

Directions:
1. To prep the strip steak: Brush both sides of the steaks with the oil and season with the steak seasoning.
2. To prep the Hasselback potatoes: Set a potato on a work surface and lay the handles of two wooden spoons lengthwise on either side of the potato. Make crosswise slits along the potato, spacing them ⅛ inch apart, being careful to not cut the potato completely through (the spoon handles will prevent you from cutting all the way through). Repeat with the remaining potatoes.
3. Rub the potatoes with the oil and season with salt.
4. In a small bowl, mix the butter, garlic, and parsley until smooth.
5. To cook the steak and potatoes: Install a crisper plate in each of the two baskets. Place the steaks in the Zone 1 basket and insert the basket in the unit. Place the potatoes in the Zone 2 basket and insert the basket in the unit.
6. Select Zone 1, select AIR FRY, set the temperature to 375°F, and set the time to 20 minutes.
7. Select Zone 2, select BAKE, set the temperature to 375°F, and set the time to 30 minutes. Select SMART FINISH.
8. Press START/PAUSE to begin cooking.
9. When both timers read 6 minutes, press START/PAUSE. Remove the Zone 1 basket and use silicone-tipped tongs to flip the steaks. Reinsert the basket in the unit. Remove the Zone 2 basket and spread the herb butter into the potatoes, being sure to work the butter in between the slices. Reinsert the basket and press START/PAUSE to resume cooking.
10. When cooking is complete, the steak should be cooked to your liking and the potato soft when pierced with a fork.
11. Remove the steaks from the basket and let rest for 5 minutes before slicing.

Nutrition:
- (Per serving) Calories: 361; Total fat: 15g; Saturated fat: 5g; Carbohydrates: 31g; Fiber: 2g; Protein: 25g; Sodium: 694mg

Air Fryer Meatloaves

Servings: 4
Cooking Time: 22 Minutes.
Ingredients:
- ⅓ cup milk
- 2 tablespoons basil pesto
- 1 egg, beaten
- 1 garlic clove, minced
- ¼ teaspoons black pepper
- 1 lb. ground beef
- ⅓ cup panko bread crumbs
- 8 pepperoni slices
- ½ cup marinara sauce, warmed
- 1 tablespoon fresh basil, chopped

Directions:
1. Mix pesto, milk, egg, garlic, and black pepper in a medium-sized bowl.
2. Stir in ground beef and bread crumbs, then mix.
3. Make the 4 small-sized loaves with this mixture and top them with 2 pepperoni slices.
4. Press the slices into the meatloaves.
5. Place the meatloaves in the two crisper plates.
6. Return the crisper plate to the Tefal Dual Zone Air Fryer.
7. Choose the Air Fry mode for Zone 1 and set the temperature to 390 degrees F and the time to 22 minutes.
8. Select the "MATCH" button to copy the settings for Zone 2.
9. Initiate cooking by pressing the START/STOP button.
10. Top them with marinara sauce and basil to serve.
11. Serve warm.

Nutrition:
- (Per serving) Calories 316 | Fat 12.2g |Sodium 587mg | Carbs 12.2g | Fiber 1g | Sugar 1.8g | Protein 25.8g

Spicy Lamb Chops

Servings: 4
Cooking Time: 15
Ingredients:
- 12 lamb chops, bone-in
- Salt and black pepper, to taste
- ½ teaspoon of lemon zest
- 1 tablespoon of lemon juice
- 1 teaspoon of paprika
- 1 teaspoon of garlic powder
- ½ teaspoon of Italian seasoning
- ¼ teaspoon of onion powder

Directions:
1. Add the lamb chops to the bowl and sprinkle salt, garlic powder, Italian seasoning, onion powder, black pepper, lemon zest, lemon juice, and paprika.
2. Rub the chops well, and divide it between both the baskets of the air fryer.
3. Set zone 1 basket to 400 degrees F, for 15 minutes at AIR FRY mode.
4. Select MATCH for zone2 basket.
5. After 10 minutes, take out the baskets and flip the chops cook for the remaining minutes, and then serve.

Nutrition:
- (Per serving) Calories 787| Fat 45.3g| Sodium1 mg | Carbs 16.1g | Fiber0.3g | Sugar 0.4g | Protein 75.3g

Pork Chops With Broccoli

Servings: 2
Cooking Time: 13 Minutes.
Ingredients:
- 2 (5 ounces) bone-in pork chops
- 2 tablespoons avocado oil
- ½ teaspoon paprika
- ½ teaspoon onion powder
- ½ teaspoon garlic powder
- 1 teaspoon salt
- 2 cups broccoli florets
- 2 garlic cloves, minced

Directions:
1. Rub the pork chops with avocado oil, garlic, paprika, and spices.
2. Add pork chop to the crisper plate of Zone 1 in the Tefal Dual Zone Air Fryer.
3. Return the crisper plate to the Air Fryer.
4. Choose the Air Fry mode for Zone 1 and set the temperature to 400 degrees F and the time to 12 minutes.
5. Add the broccoli to the Zone 2 drawer and return it to the unit.
6. Choose the Air Fry mode for Zone 2 with 375 degrees F and the time to 13 minutes.
7. Press the SYNC button to sync the finish time for both Zones.
8. Initiate cooking by pressing the START/STOP button.
9. Flip the pork once cooked halfway through.
10. Cut the hardened butter into the cubes and place them on top of the pork chops.
11. Serve warm with crispy broccoli florets

Nutrition:
- (Per serving) Calories 410 | Fat 17.8g |Sodium 619mg | Carbs 21g | Fiber 1.4g | Sugar 1.8g | Protein 38.4g

Honey Glazed Bbq Pork Ribs

Servings: 4
Cooking Time: 30 Minutes
Ingredients:
- 2 pounds pork ribs
- ¼ cup honey, divided
- 1 cup BBQ sauce
- ½ teaspoon garlic powder
- 2 tablespoons tomato ketchup
- 1 tablespoon Worcestershire sauce
- 1 tablespoon low-sodium soy sauce
- Freshly ground white pepper, as required

Directions:
1. In a bowl, mix together honey and the remaining ingredients except pork ribs.
2. Add the pork ribs and coat with the mixture generously.
3. Refrigerate to marinate for about 20 minutes.
4. Grease each basket of "Zone 1" and "Zone 2" of Tefal 2-Basket Air Fryer.
5. Press "Zone 1" and "Zone 2" and then rotate the knob for each zone to select "Air Fry".
6. Set the temperature to 355 degrees F/ 180 degrees C for both zones and then set the time for 5 minutes to preheat.
7. After preheating, arrange the ribs into the basket of each zone.
8. Slide each basket into Air Fryer and set the time for 26 minutes.
9. While cooking, flip the ribs once halfway through.
10. After cooking time is completed, remove the ribs from Air Fryer and place onto serving plates.
11. Drizzle with the remaining honey and serve immediately.

Beef Cheeseburgers

Servings: 4
Cooking Time: 13 Minutes.
Ingredients:
- 1 lb. ground beef
- Salt, to taste
- 2 garlic cloves, minced
- 1 tablespoon soy sauce
- Black pepper, to taste
- 4 American cheese slices
- 4 hamburger buns
- Mayonnaise, to serve
- Lettuce, to serve
- Sliced tomatoes, to serve
- Sliced red onion, to serve

Directions:
1. Mix beef with soy sauce and garlic in a large bowl.
2. Make 4 patties of 4 inches in diameter.
3. Rub them with salt and black pepper on both sides.
4. Place the 2 patties in each of the crisper plate.
5. Return the crisper plate to the Tefal Dual Zone Air Fryer.
6. Choose the Air Fry mode for Zone 1 and set the temperature to 390 degrees F and the time to 13 minutes.
7. Select the "MATCH" button to copy the settings for Zone 2.
8. Initiate cooking by pressing the START/STOP button.
9. Flip each patty once cooked halfway through, and resume cooking.
10. Add each patty to the hamburger buns along with mayo, tomatoes, onions, and lettuce.
11. Serve.

Nutrition:
- (Per serving) Calories 437 | Fat 28g |Sodium 1221mg | Carbs 22.3g | Fiber 0.9g | Sugar 8g | Protein 30.3g

Sumptuous Pizza Tortilla Rolls

Servings: 4
Cooking Time: 6 Minutes
Ingredients:
- 1 teaspoon butter
- ½ medium onion, slivered
- ½ red or green pepper, julienned
- 110 g fresh white mushrooms, chopped
- 120 ml pizza sauce
- 8 flour tortillas
- 8 thin slices wafer-thinham
- 24 pepperoni slices
- 235 ml shredded Mozzarella cheese
- Cooking spray

Directions:
1. Preheat the air fryer to 200°C.
2. Put butter, onions, pepper, and mushrooms in a baking pan. Bake in the preheated air fryer for 3 minutes. Stir and cook 3 to 4 minutes longer until just crisp and tender. Remove pan and set aside.
3. To assemble rolls, spread about 2 teaspoons of pizza sauce on one half of each tortilla. Top with a slice of ham and 3 slices of pepperoni. Divide sautéed vegetables among tortillas and top with cheese.
4. Roll up tortillas, secure with toothpicks if needed, and spray with oil.
5. Put the rolls in the two air fryer drawers and air fry for 4 minutes. Turn and air fry 4 minutes, until heated through and lightly browned.
6. Serve immediately.

Roasted Beef

Servings: 8
Cooking Time: 50 Minutes
Ingredients:
- 1 (1-pound) beef roast
- Salt and ground black pepper, as required

Directions:
1. Grease each basket of "Zone 1" and "Zone 2" of Tefal 2-Basket Air Fryer.
2. Press "Zone 1" and "Zone 2" and then rotate the knob for each zone to select "Roast".
3. Set the temperature to 350 degrees F/ 175 degrees C for both zones and then set the time for 5 minutes to preheat.
4. Rub ach roast with salt and black pepper generously.
5. After preheating, arrange the roast into the basket of each zone.
6. Slide each basket into Air Fryer and set the time for 50 minutes.
7. After cooking time is completed, remove each roast from Air Fryer and place onto a platter for about 10 minutes before slicing.
8. With a sharp knife, cut each roast into desired-sized slices and serve.

Bo Luc Lac

Servings: 4
Cooking Time: 8 Minutes
Ingredients:
- For the Meat:
- 2 teaspoons soy sauce
- 4 garlic cloves, minced
- 1 teaspoon coarse or flaky salt
- 2 teaspoons sugar
- ¼ teaspoon ground black pepper
- 1 teaspoon toasted sesame oil
- 680 g top rump steak, cut into 1-inch cubes
- Cooking spray
- For the Salad:
- 1 head butterhead lettuce, leaves separated and torn into large pieces
- 60 ml fresh mint leaves
- 120 ml halved baby plum tomatoes
- ½ red onion, halved and thinly sliced
- 2 tablespoons apple cider vinegar
- 1 garlic clove, minced
- 2 teaspoons sugar
- ¼ teaspoon coarse or flaky salt
- ¼ teaspoon ground black pepper
- 2 tablespoons vegetable oil
- For Serving:
- Lime wedges, for garnish
- Coarse salt and freshly cracked black pepper, to taste

Directions:
1. Combine the ingredients for the meat, except for the steak, in a large bowl. Stir to mix well.
2. Dunk the steak cubes in the bowl and press to coat. Wrap the bowl in plastic and marinate under room temperature for at least 30 minutes.
3. Preheat the air fryer to 232°C. Spritz the two air fryer drawers with cooking spray.
4. Discard the marinade and transfer the steak cubes in the two preheated air fryer drawers.
5. Air fry for 4 minutes or until the steak cubes are lightly browned but still have a little pink. Shake the drawers halfway through the cooking time.
6. Meanwhile, combine the ingredients for the salad in a separate large bowl. Toss to mix well.
7. Pour the salad in a large serving bowl and top with the steak cubes. Squeeze the lime wedges over and sprinkle with salt and black pepper before serving.

Mustard Rubbed Lamb Chops

Servings: 4
Cooking Time: 31 Minutes.
Ingredients:
- 1 teaspoon Dijon mustard
- 1 teaspoon olive oil
- ½ teaspoon soy sauce
- ½ teaspoon garlic, minced
- ½ teaspoon cumin powder
- ½ teaspoon cayenne pepper
- ½ teaspoon Italian spice blend
- ⅛ teaspoon salt
- 4 pieces of lamb chops

Directions:
1. Mix Dijon mustard, soy sauce, olive oil, garlic, cumin powder, cayenne pepper, Italian spice blend, and salt in a medium bowl and mix well.
2. Place lamb chops into a Ziploc bag and pour in the marinade.
3. Press the air out of the bag and seal tightly.
4. Press the marinade around the lamb chops to coat.
5. Keep then in the fridge and marinate for at least 30 minutes, up to overnight.
6. Place 2 chops in each of the crisper plate and spray them with cooking oil.
7. Return the crisper plate to the Tefal Dual Zone Air Fryer.
8. Select the Roast mode for Zone 1 and set the temperature to 350 degrees F and the time to 27 minutes.
9. Select the "MATCH" button to copy the settings for Zone 2.
10. Initiate cooking by pressing the START/STOP button.
11. Flip the chops once cooked halfway through, and resume cooking.
12. Switch the Roast mode to Max Crisp mode and cook for 5 minutes.
13. Serve warm.

Nutrition:
- (Per serving) Calories 264 | Fat 17g | Sodium 129mg | Carbs 0.9g | Fiber 0.3g | Sugar 0g | Protein 27g

Steak Bites With Cowboy Butter

Servings: 4
Cooking Time: 20 Minutes
Ingredients:
- 455g steak sirloin
- Cooking spray
- Cowboy butter sauce
- 1 stick salted butter melted
- 1 tablespoon lemon zest
- 1 tablespoon lemon juice
- ½ teaspoon garlic powder
- ¼ teaspoon red pepper flakes
- ½ teaspoon sea salt
- ½ teaspoon black pepper
- ½ tablespoon Dijon mustard
- ½ teaspoon Worcestershire sauce
- 1 tablespoon parsley freshly chopped

Directions:
1. Mix all the cowboy butter ingredients in a bowl.
2. Stir in steak cubes and mix well.
3. Cover and marinate in the refrigerator for 1 hour.
4. Divide the steak cubes in the air fryer baskets then use cooking spray.
5. Return the air fryer basket 1 to Zone 1, and basket 2 to Zone 2 of the Tefal 2-Basket Air Fryer.
6. Choose the "Air Fry" mode for Zone 1 at 400 degrees F and 15 minutes of cooking time.
7. Select the "MATCH COOK" option to copy the settings for Zone 2.
8. Initiate cooking by pressing the START/PAUSE BUTTON.
9. Serve warm.

Cinnamon-apple Pork Chops

Servings: 4
Cooking Time: 10 Minutes
Ingredients:
- 2 tablespoons butter
- 4 boneless pork loin chops
- 3 tablespoons brown sugar
- 1 teaspoon ground cinnamon
- ½ teaspoon ground nutmeg
- ¼ teaspoon salt
- 4 medium tart apples, sliced
- 2 tablespoons chopped pecans

Directions:
1. Mix butter, brown sugar, cinnamon, nutmeg, and salt in a bowl.
2. Rub this mixture over the pork chops and place them in the air fryer baskets.
3. Top them with apples and pecans.
4. Return the air fryer basket 1 to Zone 1, and basket 2 to Zone 2 of the Tefal 2-Basket Air Fryer.
5. Choose the "Air Fry" mode for Zone 1 at 375 degrees F and 10 minutes of cooking time.
6. Select the "MATCH COOK" option to copy the settings for Zone 2.
7. Initiate cooking by pressing the START/PAUSE BUTTON.
8. Serve warm.

Sausage Meatballs

Servings: 24
Cooking Time: 30 Minutes
Ingredients:
- 1 egg, lightly beaten
- 900g pork sausage
- 29g breadcrumbs
- 100g pimientos, drained & diced
- 1 tsp curry powder
- 1 tbsp garlic, minced
- 30ml olive oil
- 1 tbsp fresh rosemary, minced
- 25g parsley, minced
- Pepper
- Salt

Directions:
1. In a bowl, add pork sausage and remaining ingredients and mix until well combined.
2. Insert a crisper plate in the Tefal air fryer baskets.
3. Make small balls from the meat mixture and place them in both baskets.
4. Select zone 1 then select "air fry" mode and set the temperature to 390 degrees F for 10 minutes. Press "match" to match zone 2 settings to zone 1. Press "start/stop" to begin.

Smothered Chops

Servings: 4
Cooking Time: 30 Minutes
Ingredients:
- 4 bone-in pork chops (230 g each)
- 2 teaspoons salt, divided
- 1½ teaspoons freshly ground black pepper, divided
- 1 teaspoon garlic powder
- 235 ml tomato purée
- 1½ teaspoons Italian seasoning
- 1 tablespoon sugar
- 1 tablespoon cornflour
- 120 ml chopped onion
- 120 ml chopped green pepper
- 1 to 2 tablespoons oil

Directions:
1. Evenly season the pork chops with 1 teaspoon salt, 1 teaspoon pepper, and the garlic powder.
2. In a medium bowl, stir together the tomato purée, Italian seasoning, sugar, remaining 1 teaspoon of salt, and remaining ½ teaspoon of pepper.
3. In a small bowl, whisk 180 ml water and the cornflour until blended. Stir this slurry into the tomato purée, with the onion and green pepper. Transfer to a baking pan.
4. Preheat the air fryer to 176°C.
5. Place the sauce in the fryer and cook for 10 minutes. Stir and cook for 10 minutes more. Remove the pan and keep warm.
6. Increase the air fryer temperature to 204°C. Line the two air fryer drawers with parchment paper.
7. Place the pork chops on the parchment and spritz with oil.
8. Cook for 5 minutes. Flip and spritz the chops with oil and cook for 5 minutes more, until the internal temperature reaches 64°C. Serve with the tomato mixture spooned on top.

Garlic-rosemary Pork Loin With Scalloped Potatoes And Cauliflower

Servings: 6
Cooking Time: 50 Minutes
Ingredients:
- FOR THE PORK LOIN
- 2 pounds pork loin roast
- 2 tablespoons vegetable oil
- 2 teaspoons dried thyme
- 2 teaspoons dried crushed rosemary
- 1 teaspoon minced garlic
- ¾ teaspoon kosher salt
- FOR THE SCALLOPED POTATOES AND CAULIFLOWER
- 1 teaspoon vegetable oil
- ¾ pound Yukon Gold potatoes, peeled and very thinly sliced
- 1½ cups cauliflower florets
- ¼ teaspoon kosher salt
- ¼ teaspoon freshly ground black pepper
- 1 tablespoon very cold unsalted butter, grated
- 3 tablespoons all-purpose flour
- 1 cup whole milk
- 1 cup shredded Gruyère cheese

Directions:
1. To prep the pork loin: Coat the pork with the oil. Season with thyme, rosemary, garlic, and salt.
2. To prep the potatoes and cauliflower: Brush the bottom and sides of the Zone 2 basket with the oil. Add one-third of the potatoes to the bottom of the basket and arrange in a single layer. Top with ½ cup of cauliflower florets. Sprinkle a third of the salt and black pepper on top. Scatter one-third of the butter on top and sprinkle on 1 tablespoon of flour. Repeat this step twice more for a total of three layers.
3. Pour the milk over the layered potatoes and cauliflower; it should just cover the top layer. Top with the Gruyère.
4. To cook the pork and scalloped vegetables: Install a crisper plate in the Zone 1 basket. Place the pork loin in the basket and insert the basket in the unit. Insert the Zone 2 basket in the unit.
5. Select Zone 1, select AIR FRY, set the temperature to 390°F, and set the time to 50 minutes.
6. Select Zone 2, select BAKE, set the temperature to 350°F, and set the time to 45 minutes. Select SMART FINISH.
7. Press START/PAUSE to begin cooking.
8. When cooking is complete, the pork will be cooked through (an instant-read thermometer should read 145°F) and the potatoes and cauliflower will be tender.
9. Let the pork rest for at least 15 minutes before slicing and serving with the scalloped vegetables.

Nutrition:
- (Per serving) Calories: 439; Total fat: 25g; Saturated fat: 10g; Carbohydrates: 17g; Fiber: 1.5g; Protein: 37g; Sodium: 431mg

Kielbasa Sausage With Pineapple And Kheema Meatloaf

Servings: 6 To 8
Cooking Time: 15 Minutes
Ingredients:
- Kielbasa Sausage with Pineapple:
- 340 g kielbasa sausage, cut into ½-inch slices
- 1 (230 g) can pineapple chunks in juice, drained
- 235 ml pepper chunks
- 1 tablespoon barbecue seasoning
- 1 tablespoon soy sauce
- Cooking spray
- Kheema Meatloaf:
- 450 g 85% lean beef mince
- 2 large eggs, lightly beaten
- 235 ml diced brown onion
- 60 ml chopped fresh coriander
- 1 tablespoon minced fresh ginger
- 1 tablespoon minced garlic
- 2 teaspoons garam masala
- 1 teaspoon coarse or flaky salt
- 1 teaspoon ground turmeric
- 1 teaspoon cayenne pepper
- ½ teaspoon ground cinnamon
- ⅛ teaspoon ground cardamom

Directions:
1. Make the Kielbasa Sausage with Pineapple :
2. Preheat the air fryer to 200°C. Spritz the zone 1 air fryer drawer with cooking spray.
3. Combine all the ingredients in a large bowl. Toss to mix well.
4. Pour the sausage mixture in the preheated zone 1 air fryer drawer.
5. Air fry for 10 minutes or until the sausage is lightly browned and the pepper and pineapple are soft. Shake the drawer halfway through. Serve immediately.
6. Make the Kheema Meatloaf :
7. In a large bowl, gently mix the beef mince, eggs, onion, coriander, ginger, garlic, garam masala, salt, turmeric, cayenne, cinnamon, and cardamom until thoroughly combined.
8. Place the seasoned meat in a baking pan. Place the pan in the zone 2 air fryer drawer. Set the temperature to 176°C for 15 minutes. Use a meat thermometer to ensure the meat loaf has reached an internal temperature of 72°C .
9. Drain the fat and liquid from the pan and let stand for 5 minutes before slicing.
10. Slice and serve hot.

Beef Ribs Ii

Servings:2
Cooking Time:1
Ingredients:
- ¼ cup olive oil
- 4 garlic cloves, minced
- ½ cup white wine vinegar
- ¼ cup soy sauce, reduced-sodium
- ¼ cup Worcestershire sauce
- 1 lemon juice
- Salt and black pepper, to taste
- 2 tablespoons of Italian seasoning
- 1 teaspoon of smoked paprika
- 2 tablespoons of mustard
- ½ cup maple syrup
- Meat Ingredients:
- Oil spray, for greasing
- 8 beef ribs lean

Directions:
1. Take a large bowl and add all the ingredients under marinade ingredients.
2. Put the marinade in a zip lock bag and add ribs to it.
3. Let it sit for 4 hours.
4. Now take out the basket of air fryer and grease the baskets with oil spray.
5. Now dived the ribs among two baskets.
6. Set it to AIR fry mode at 220 degrees F for 30 minutes.
7. Select Pause and take out the baskets.
8. Afterward, flip the ribs and cook for 30 minutes at 250 degrees F.
9. Once done, serve the juicy and tender ribs.
10. Enjoy.

Nutrition:
- (Per serving) Calories 1927| Fat116g| Sodium 1394mg | Carbs 35.2g | Fiber 1.3g| Sugar29 g | Protein 172.3g

Bbq Pork Spare Ribs

Servings: 8
Cooking Time: 30 Minutes
Ingredients:
- ½ cup honey, divided
- 1½ cups BBQ sauce
- 4 tablespoons tomato ketchup
- 2 tablespoons Worcestershire sauce
- 2 tablespoons low-sodium soy sauce
- 1 teaspoon garlic powder
- Freshly ground white pepper, as required
- 3½ pounds pork ribs

Directions:
1. In a bowl, mix together 6 tablespoons of honey and the remaining ingredients except pork ribs.
2. Add the pork ribs and coat with the mixture generously.
3. Refrigerate to marinate for about 20 minutes.
4. Grease each basket of "Zone 1" and "Zone 2" of Tefal 2-Basket Air Fryer.
5. Press "Zone 1" and "Zone 2" and then rotate the knob for each zone to select "Air Fry".
6. Set the temperature to 355 degrees F/ 180 degrees C for both zones and then set the time for 5 minutes to preheat.
7. After preheating, arrange the ribs into the basket of each zone.
8. Slide each basket into Air Fryer and set the time for 26 minutes.
9. While cooking, flip the ribs once halfway through.
10. After cooking time is completed, remove the ribs from Air Fryer and place onto serving plates.
11. Drizzle with the remaining honey and serve immediately.

Sausage-stuffed Peppers

Servings: 6
Cooking Time: 28 To 30 Minutes
Ingredients:
- Avocado oil spray
- 230 g Italian-seasoned sausage, casings removed
- 120 ml chopped mushrooms
- 60 ml diced onion
- 1 teaspoon Italian seasoning
- Sea salt and freshly ground black pepper, to taste
- 235 ml keto-friendly marinara sauce
- 3 peppers, halved and seeded
- 85 g low-moisture Mozzarella or other melting cheese, shredded

Directions:
1. Spray a large skillet with oil and place it over medium-high heat. Add the sausage and cook for 5 minutes, breaking up the meat with a wooden spoon. Add the mushrooms, onion, and Italian seasoning, and season with salt and pepper. Cook for 5 minutes more. Stir in the marinara sauce and cook until heated through.
2. Scoop the sausage filling into the pepper halves.
3. Set the air fryer to 176°C. Arrange the peppers in a single layer in the two air fryer drawers. Air fry for 15 minutes.
4. Top the stuffed peppers with the cheese and air fry for 3 to 5 minutes more, until the cheese is melted and the peppers are tender.

Cinnamon-beef Kofta

Servings: 12 Koftas
Cooking Time: 13 Minutes
Ingredients:
- 680 g lean beef mince
- 1 teaspoon onion granules
- ¾ teaspoon ground cinnamon
- ¾ teaspoon ground dried turmeric
- 1 teaspoon ground cumin
- ¾ teaspoon salt
- ¼ teaspoon cayenne
- 12 (3½- to 4-inch-long) cinnamon sticks
- Cooking spray

Directions:
1. Preheat the air fryer to 192°C. Spritz the two air fryer drawers with cooking spray.
2. Combine all the ingredients, except for the cinnamon sticks, in a large bowl. Toss to mix well.
3. Divide and shape the mixture into 12 balls, then wrap each ball around each cinnamon stick and leave a quarter of the length uncovered.
4. Arrange the beef-cinnamon sticks in the preheated air fryer and spritz with cooking spray.
5. Air fry for 13 minutes or until the beef is browned. Flip the sticks halfway through.
6. Serve immediately.

Pigs In A Blanket With Spinach-artichoke Stuffed Mushrooms

Servings: 4
Cooking Time: 15 Minutes
Ingredients:
- FOR THE PIGS IN A BLANKET
- Half an 8-ounce tube refrigerated crescent roll dough
- 4 hot dogs
- ½ teaspoon everything bagel seasoning (optional)
- FOR THE STUFFED MUSHROOMS
- 1 cup frozen chopped spinach, thawed and drained
- 1 (14-ounce) can artichoke hearts, drained and chopped
- 2 ounces (¼ cup) cream cheese, at room temperature
- ¼ cup grated Parmesan cheese
- ½ teaspoon garlic powder
- 1 (8-ounce) package whole cremini mushrooms, stems removed

Directions:
1. To prep the pigs in a blanket: Unroll the crescent roll dough. It will be scored into 4 triangular pieces, but leave them in place and pinch together at the seams to form 1 large square of dough. Cut the dough into 4 strips.
2. Wrap one strip of dough around each hot dog, starting with a short end of the strips and wrapping in a spiral motion around the hot dog. If desired, sprinkle each pig in a blanket with everything bagel seasoning.
3. To prep the stuffed mushrooms: In a medium bowl, combine the spinach, artichoke hearts, cream cheese, Parmesan, and garlic powder. Stuff about 1 tablespoon of filling into each mushroom cap.
4. To cook the pigs in a blanket and mushrooms: Install a crisper plate in each of the two baskets. Place the pigs in a blanket in the Zone 1 basket and insert the basket in the unit. Place the mushrooms in the Zone 2 basket and insert the basket in the unit.
5. Select Zone 1, select AIR FRY, set the temperature to 370°F, and set the time to 8 minutes.
6. Select Zone 2, select BAKE, set the temperature to 370°F, and set the time to 15 minutes. Select SMART FINISH.
7. Press START/PAUSE to begin cooking.
8. When cooking is complete, the crescent roll dough should be cooked through and golden brown, and the mushrooms should be tender.

Nutrition:
- (Per serving) Calories: 371; Total fat: 25g; Saturated fat: 11g; Carbohydrates: 22g; Fiber: 2.5g; Protein: 14g; Sodium: 1,059mg

Nigerian Peanut-crusted Bavette Steak

Servings: 4
Cooking Time: 8 Minutes
Ingredients:
- Suya Spice Mix:
- 60 ml dry-roasted peanuts
- 1 teaspoon cumin seeds
- 1 teaspoon garlic powder
- 1 teaspoon smoked paprika
- ½ teaspoon ground ginger
- 1 teaspoon coarse or flaky salt
- ½ teaspoon cayenne pepper
- Steak:
- 450 g bavette or skirt steak
- 2 tablespoons vegetable oil

Directions:
1. For the spice mix: In a clean coffee grinder or spice mill, combine the peanuts and cumin seeds. Process until you get a coarse powder. 2. Pour the peanut mixture into a small bowl, add the garlic powder, paprika, ginger, salt, and cayenne, and stir to combine. This recipe makes about 120 ml suya spice mix. Store leftovers in an airtight container in a cool, dry place for up to 1 month. 3. For the steak: Cut the steak into ½-inch-thick slices, cutting against the grain and at a slight angle. Place the beef strips in a resealable plastic bag and add the oil and 2½ to 3 tablespoons of the spice mixture. Seal the bag and massage to coat all of the meat with the oil and spice mixture. Marinate at room temperature for 30 minutes or in the refrigerator for up to 24 hours. 4. Place the beef strips in the zone 1 air fryer drawer. Set the temperature to 204°C for 8 minutes, turning the strips halfway through the cooking time. 5. Transfer the meat to a serving platter. Sprinkle with additional spice mix, if desired.

Goat Cheese-stuffed Bavette Steak

Servings: 6
Cooking Time: 14 Minutes
Ingredients:
- 450 g bavette or skirt steak
- 1 tablespoon avocado oil
- ½ teaspoon sea salt
- ½ teaspoon garlic powder
- ¼ teaspoon freshly ground black pepper
- 60 g goat cheese, crumbled
- 235 ml baby spinach, chopped

Directions:
1. Place the steak in a large zip-top bag or between two pieces of plastic wrap. Using a meat mallet or heavy-bottomed skillet, pound the steak to an even ¼-inch thickness.
2. Brush both sides of the steak with the avocado oil.
3. Mix the salt, garlic powder, and pepper in a small dish. Sprinkle this mixture over both sides of the steak.
4. Sprinkle the goat cheese over top, and top that with the spinach.
5. Starting at one of the long sides, roll the steak up tightly. Tie the rolled steak with kitchen string at 3-inch intervals.
6. Set the zone 1 air fryer drawer to 204°C. Place the steak roll-up in the zone 1 air fryer drawer. Air fry for 7 minutes. Flip the steak and cook for an additional 7 minutes, until an instant-read thermometer reads 49°C for medium-rare.

Garlic Sirloin Steak

Servings: 4
Cooking Time: 10 Minutes
Ingredients:
- 4 sirloin steak
- 30ml olive oil
- 28g steak sauce
- ½ tsp ground coriander
- 1 tsp garlic, minced
- 1 tbsp thyme, chopped
- Pepper
- Salt

Directions:
1. In a bowl, mix steak with thyme, oil, steak sauce, coriander, garlic, pepper, and salt. Cover and set aside for 2 hours.
2. Insert a crisper plate in Tefal air fryer baskets.
3. Place the marinated steaks in both baskets.
4. Select zone 1 then select air fry mode and set the temperature to 360 degrees F for 10 minutes. Press "match" and then "start/stop" to begin.

Lamb Shank With Mushroom Sauce

Servings: 4
Cooking Time: 35 Minutes.
Ingredients:
- 20 mushrooms, chopped
- 2 red bell pepper, chopped
- 2 red onion, chopped
- 1 cup red wine
- 4 leeks, chopped
- 6 tablespoons balsamic vinegar
- 2 teaspoons black pepper
- 2 teaspoons salt
- 3 tablespoons fresh rosemary
- 6 garlic cloves
- 4 lamb shanks
- 3 tablespoons olive oil

Directions:
1. Season the lamb shanks with salt, pepper, rosemary, and 1 teaspoon of olive oil.
2. Set half of the shanks in each of the crisper plate.
3. Return the crisper plate to the Tefal Dual Zone Air Fryer.
4. Choose the Air Fry mode for Zone 1 and set the temperature to 390 degrees F and the time to 25 minutes.
5. Select the "MATCH" button to copy the settings for Zone 2.
6. Initiate cooking by pressing the START/STOP button.
7. Flip the shanks halfway through, and resume cooking.
8. Meanwhile, add and heat the remaining olive oil in a skillet.
9. Add onion and garlic to sauté for 5 minutes.
10. Add in mushrooms and cook for 5 minutes.
11. Add red wine and cook until it is absorbed
12. Stir all the remaining vegetables along with black pepper and salt.
13. Cook until vegetables are al dente.
14. Serve the air fried shanks with sautéed vegetable fry.

Nutrition:
- (Per serving) Calories 352 | Fat 9.1g |Sodium 1294mg | Carbs 3.9g | Fiber 1g | Sugar 1g | Protein 61g

Tasty Lamb Patties

Servings: 8
Cooking Time: 12 Minutes
Ingredients:
- 900g ground lamb
- 1 tbsp ground coriander
- 4g fresh parsley, chopped
- 1 tsp garlic, minced
- ½ tsp cinnamon
- 1 tsp paprika
- 1 tbsp ground cumin
- Pepper
- Salt

Directions:
1. Add ground meat and remaining ingredients into a bowl and mix until well combined.
2. Insert a crisper plate in the Tefal air fryer baskets.
3. Make patties from the meat mixture and place in both baskets.
4. Select zone 1, then select "air fry" mode and set the temperature to 390 degrees F for 12 minutes. Press "match" to match zone 2 settings to zone 1. Press "start/stop" to begin. Turn halfway through.

Sausage And Pork Meatballs

Servings: 8
Cooking Time: 8 To 12 Minutes
Ingredients:
- 1 large egg
- 1 teaspoon gelatin
- 450 g pork mince
- 230 g Italian-seasoned sausage, casings removed, crumbled
- 80 ml Parmesan cheese
- 60 ml finely diced onion
- 1 tablespoon tomato paste
- 1 teaspoon minced garlic
- 1 teaspoon dried oregano
- ¼ teaspoon red pepper flakes
- Sea salt and freshly ground black pepper, to taste
- Keto-friendly marinara sauce, for serving

Directions:
1. Beat the egg in a small bowl and sprinkle with the gelatin. Allow to sit for 5 minutes.
2. In a large bowl, combine the pork mince, sausage, Parmesan, onion, tomato paste, garlic, oregano, and red pepper flakes. Season with salt and black pepper.
3. Stir the gelatin mixture, then add it to the other ingredients and, using clean hands, mix to ensure that everything is well combined. Form into 1½-inch round meatballs.
4. Set the air fryer to 204°C. Place the meatballs in the two air fryer drawers in a single layer. Air fry for 5 minutes. Flip and cook for 3 to 7 minutes more, or until an instant-read thermometer reads 72°C.

Blue Cheese Steak Salad

Servings: 4
Cooking Time: 22 Minutes
Ingredients:
- 2 tablespoons balsamic vinegar
- 2 tablespoons red wine vinegar
- 1 tablespoon Dijon mustard
- 1 tablespoon granulated sweetener
- 1 teaspoon minced garlic
- Sea salt and freshly ground black pepper, to taste
- 180 ml extra-virgin olive oil
- 450 g boneless rump steak
- Avocado oil spray
- 1 small red onion, cut into ¼-inch-thick rounds
- 170 g baby spinach
- 120 ml cherry tomatoes, halved
- 85 g blue cheese, crumbled

Directions:
1. In a blender, combine the balsamic vinegar, red wine vinegar, Dijon mustard, sweetener, and garlic. Season with salt and pepper and process until smooth. With the blender running, drizzle in the olive oil. Process until well combined. Transfer to a jar with a tight-fitting lid, and refrigerate until ready to serve.
2. Season the steak with salt and pepper and let sit at room temperature for at least 45 minutes, time permitting.
3. Set the zone 1 air fryer drawer to 204°C. Spray the steak with oil and place it in the zone 1 air fryer drawer. Spray the onion slices with oil and place them in the zone 2 air fryer drawer.
4. In zone 1, air fry for 6 minutes. Flip the steak and spray it with more oil. Air fry for 6 minutes more for medium-rare or until the steak is done to your liking.
5. In zone 2, cook at 204°C for 5 minutes. Flip the onion slices and spray them with more oil. Air fry for 5 minutes more.
6. Transfer the steak to a plate, tent with a piece of aluminum foil, and allow it to rest. Slice the steak diagonally into thin strips. Place the spinach, cherry tomatoes, onion slices, and steak in a large bowl. Toss with the desired amount of dressing. Sprinkle with crumbled blue cheese and serve.

Bacon-wrapped Filet Mignon

Servings: 4
Cooking Time: 15 Minutes
Ingredients:
- 4 bacon slices
- 4 (4-ounce) filet mignon
- Salt and ground black pepper, as required
- Olive oil cooking spray

Directions:
1. Wrap 1 bacon slice around each filet mignon and secure with toothpicks.
2. Spray the filet mignon with cooking spray evenly. Season the filets with salt and black pepper lightly.
3. Grease each basket of "Zone 1" and "Zone 2" of Tefal 2-Basket Air Fryer.
4. Press "Zone 1" and "Zone 2" and then rotate the knob for each zone to select "Air Fry".
5. Set the temperature to 400 degrees F/ 200 degrees C for both zones and then set the time for 5 minutes to preheat.
6. After preheating, arrange 2 filets into the basket of each zone.
7. Slide each basket into Air Fryer and set the time for 15 minutes.
8. While cooking, flip the filets once halfway through.
9. After cooking time is completed, remove the filets from Air Fryer and serve hot.

Italian Sausage And Cheese Meatballs

Servings: 4
Cooking Time: 20 Minutes
Ingredients:
- 230 g sausage meat with Italian seasoning added to taste
- 230 g 85% lean beef mince
- 120 ml shredded sharp Cheddar cheese
- ½ teaspoon onion granules
- ½ teaspoon garlic powder
- ½ teaspoon black pepper

Directions:
1. In a large bowl, gently mix the sausage meat, beef mince, cheese, onion granules, garlic powder, and pepper until well combined.
2. Form the mixture into 16 meatballs. Place the meatballs in a single layer in the two air fryer drawers. Set the air fryer to 176°C for 20 minutes, turning the meatballs halfway through the cooking time. Use a meat thermometer to ensure the meatballs have reached an internal temperature of 72°C.

Vegetables And Sides Recipes

Mixed Air Fry Veggies

Servings: 4
Cooking Time: 25 Minutes
Ingredients:
- 2 cups carrots, cubed
- 2 cups potatoes, cubed
- 2 cups shallots, cubed
- 2 cups zucchini, diced
- 2 cups yellow squash, cubed
- Salt and black pepper, to taste
- 1 tablespoon Italian seasoning
- 2 tablespoons ranch seasoning
- 4 tablespoons olive oil

Directions:
1. Take a large bowl and add all the veggies to it.
2. Season the veggies with salt, pepper, Italian seasoning, ranch seasoning, and olive oil.
3. Toss all the ingredients well.
4. Divide the veggies into both the baskets of the air fryer.
5. Set zone 1 basket to AIR FRY mode at 360 degrees F for 25 minutes.
6. Select the MATCH button for the zone 2 basket.
7. Once it is cooked and done, serve, and enjoy.

Zucchini With Stuffing

Servings: 3
Cooking Time: 20
Ingredients:
- 1 cup quinoa, rinsed
- 1 cup black olives
- 6 medium zucchinis, about 2 pounds
- 2 cups cannellini beans, drained
- 1 white onion, chopped
- ¼ cup almonds, chopped
- 4 cloves of garlic, chopped
- 4 tablespoons olive oil
- 1 cup of water
- 2 cups Parmesan cheese, for topping

Directions:
1. First wash the zucchini and cut it lengthwise.
2. Take a skillet and heat oil in it
3. Sauté the onion in olive oil for a few minutes.
4. Then add the quinoa and water and let it cook for 8 minutes with the lid on the top.
5. Transfer the quinoa to a bowl and add all remaining ingredients excluding zucchini and Parmesan cheese.
6. Scoop out the seeds of zucchinis.
7. Fill the cavity of zucchinis with bowl mixture.
8. Top it with a handful of Parmesan cheese.
9. Arrange 4 zucchinis in both air fryer baskets.
10. Select zone1 basket at AIR FRY for 20 minutes and adjusting the temperature to 390 degrees F.
11. Use the Match button to select the same setting for zone 2.
12. Serve and enjoy.

Nutrition:
- (Per serving) Calories 1171| Fat 48.6g| Sodium 1747mg | Carbs 132.4g | Fiber 42.1g | Sugar 11.5g | Protein 65.7g

Green Beans With Baked Potatoes

Servings: 2
Cooking Time: 45 Minutes
Ingredients:
- 2 cups green beans
- 2 large potatoes, cubed
- 3 tablespoons olive oil
- 1 teaspoon seasoned salt
- ½ teaspoon chili powder
- ⅙ teaspoon garlic powder
- ¼ teaspoon onion powder

Directions:
1. Take a large bowl and pour olive oil into it.
2. Add all the seasoning in the olive oil and whisk it well.
3. Toss the green beans in and mix well and then transfer to zone 1 basket of the air fryer.
4. Season the potatoes with the oil seasoning and add them to the zone 2 basket.
5. Press the Sync button.
6. Once the cooking cycle is complete, take out and serve.

Pepper Poppers

Servings: 24
Cooking Time: 20 Minutes
Ingredients:
- 8 ounces cream cheese, softened
- ¾ cup shredded cheddar cheese
- ¾ cup shredded Monterey Jack cheese
- 6 bacon strips, cooked and crumbled
- ¼ teaspoon salt
- ¼ teaspoon garlic powder
- ¼ teaspoon chili powder
- ¼ teaspoon smoked paprika
- 1-pound fresh jalapeño peppers, halved lengthwise and deseeded
- ½ cup dry breadcrumbs
- Sour cream, French onion dip, or ranch salad dressing (optional)

Directions:
1. In a large bowl, combine the cheeses, bacon, and seasonings| mix well. Spoon 1½ to 2 tablespoons of the mixture into each pepper half. Roll them in the breadcrumbs.
2. Place a crisper plate in each drawer. Put the prepared peppers in a single layer in each drawer. Insert the drawers into the unit.
3. Select zone 1, then AIR FRY, then set the temperature to 360 degrees F/ 180 degrees C with a 20-minute timer. To match zone 2 settings to zone 1, choose MATCH. To begin, select START/STOP.
4. Remove the peppers from the drawers after the timer has finished.

Kale And Spinach Chips

Servings: 2
Cooking Time: 6 Minutes
Ingredients:
- 2 cups spinach, torn in pieces and stem removed
- 2 cups kale, torn in pieces, stems removed
- 1 tablespoon olive oil
- Sea salt, to taste
- ⅓ cup Parmesan cheese

Directions:
1. Take a bowl and add spinach to it.
2. Take another bowl and add kale to it.
3. Season both of them with olive oil and sea salt.
4. Add the kale to the zone 1 basket and spinach to the zone 2 basket.
5. Select AIR FRY mode for zone 1 at 350 degrees F/ 175 degrees C for 6 minutes.
6. Set zone 2 to AIR FRY mode at 350 degrees F/ 175 degrees C for 5 minutes.
7. Once done, take out the crispy chips and sprinkle Parmesan cheese on top. 8. Serve and Enjoy.

Fresh Mix Veggies In Air Fryer

Servings: 4
Cooking Time: 12 Minutes
Ingredients:
- 1 cup cauliflower florets
- 1 cup carrots, peeled chopped
- 1 cup broccoli florets
- 2 tablespoons avocado oil
- Salt, to taste
- ½ teaspoon chili powder
- ½ teaspoon garlic powder
- ½ teaspoon herbs de Provence
- 1 cup Parmesan cheese

Directions:
1. Take a bowl, and add all the veggies to it.
2. Toss and then season the veggies with salt, chili powder, garlic powder, and herbs de Provence.
3. Toss it all well and then drizzle avocado oil.
4. Make sure the ingredients are coated well.
5. Distribute the veggies among both baskets of the air fryer.
6. Turn on the START/STOP button and set it to AIR FRY mode at 390 degrees F/ 200 degrees C for 10-12 minutes.
7. For the zone 2 basket setting, press the MATCH button.
8. After 8 minutes of cooking, press the START/STOP button and then take out the baskets and sprinkle Parmesan cheese on top of the veggies.
9. Then let the cooking cycle complete for the next 3-4 minutes.
10. Once done, serve.

Brussels Sprouts

Servings: 2
Cooking Time: 20 Minutes
Ingredients:
- 2 pounds Brussels sprouts
- 2 tablespoons avocado oil
- Salt and pepper, to taste
- 1 cup pine nuts, roasted

Directions:
1. Trim the bottom of the Brussels sprouts.
2. Take a bowl and combine the avocado oil, salt, and black pepper.
3. Toss the Brussels sprouts into the bowl and mix well.
4. Divide the mixture into both air fryer baskets.
5. For zone 1 set to AIR FRY mode for 20 minutes at 390 degrees F/ 200 degrees C.
6. Select the MATCH button for the zone 2 basket.
7. Once the Brussels sprouts get crisp and tender, take out and serve.

Fried Asparagus

Servings: 4
Cooking Time: 6 Minutes
Ingredients:
- ¼ cup mayonnaise
- 4 teaspoons olive oil
- 1½ teaspoons grated lemon zest
- 1 garlic clove, minced
- ½ teaspoon pepper
- ¼ teaspoon seasoned salt
- 1-pound fresh asparagus, trimmed
- 2 tablespoons shredded parmesan cheese
- Lemon wedges (optional)

Directions:
1. In a large bowl, combine the first 6 ingredients.
2. Add the asparagus| toss to coat.
3. Put a crisper plate in both drawers. Put the asparagus in a single layer in each drawer. Top with the parmesan cheese. Place the drawers into the unit.
4. Select zone 1, then AIR FRY, then set the temperature to 375 degrees F/ 190 degrees C with a 6-minute timer. To match zone 2 settings to zone 1, choose MATCH. To begin, select START/STOP.
5. Remove the asparagus from the drawers after the timer has finished.

Flavourful Mexican Cauliflower

Servings: 4
Cooking Time: 12 Minutes
Ingredients:
- 1 medium cauliflower head, cut into florets
- ½ tsp turmeric
- 1 tsp onion powder
- 2 tsp garlic powder
- 2 tsp parsley
- 1 lime juice
- 30ml olive oil
- 1 tsp chilli powder
- 1 tsp cumin
- Pepper
- Salt

Directions:
1. In a bowl, toss cauliflower florets with onion powder, garlic powder, parsley, oil, chilli powder, turmeric, cumin, pepper, and salt.
2. Insert a crisper plate in the Tefal air fryer baskets.
3. Add cauliflower florets in both baskets.
4. Select zone 1, then select "air fry" mode and set the temperature to 390 degrees F for 12 minutes. Press "match" to match zone 2 settings to zone 1. Press "start/stop" to begin. Stir halfway through.
5. Drizzle lime juice over cauliflower florets.

Nutrition:
- (Per serving) Calories 108 | Fat 7.4g |Sodium 91mg | Carbs 10g | Fiber 4.1g | Sugar 4.1g | Protein 3.4g

Garlic-herb Fried Squash

Servings: 4
Cooking Time: 15 Minutes
Ingredients:
- 5 cups halved small pattypan squash (about 1¼ pounds)
- 1 tablespoon olive oil
- 2 garlic cloves, minced
- ½ teaspoon salt
- ¼ teaspoon dried oregano
- ¼ teaspoon dried thyme
- ¼ teaspoon pepper
- 1 tablespoon minced fresh parsley, for serving

Directions:
1. Place the squash in a large bowl.
2. Mix the oil, garlic, salt, oregano, thyme, and pepper| drizzle over the squash. Toss to coat.
3. Place a crisper plate in both drawers. Put the squash in a single layer in each drawer. Insert the drawers into the unit.
4. Select zone 1, then AIR FRY, then set the temperature to 360 degrees F/ 180 degrees C with a 6-minute timer. To match zone 2 settings to zone 1, choose MATCH. To begin, select START/STOP.
5. Remove the squash from the drawers after the timer has finished. Sprinkle with the parsley.

Beets With Orange Gremolata And Goat's Cheese

Servings: 12
Cooking Time: 45 Minutes
Ingredients:
- 3 medium fresh golden beets (about 1 pound)
- 3 medium fresh beets (about 1 pound)
- 2 tablespoons lime juice
- 2 tablespoons orange juice
- ½ teaspoon fine sea salt
- 1 tablespoon minced fresh parsley
- 1 tablespoon minced fresh sage
- 1 garlic clove, minced
- 1 teaspoon grated orange zest
- 3 tablespoons crumbled goat's cheese
- 2 tablespoons sunflower kernels

Directions:
1. Scrub the beets and trim the tops by 1 inch.
2. Place the beets on a double thickness of heavy-duty foil . Fold the foil around the beets, sealing tightly.
3. Place a crisper plate in both drawers. Put the beets in a single layer in each drawer. Insert the drawers into the unit.
4. Select zone 1, then AIR FRY, then set the temperature to 360 degrees F/ 180 degrees C with a 45-minute timer. To match zone 2 settings to zone 1, choose MATCH. To begin, select START/STOP.
5. Remove the beets from the drawers after the timer has finished. Peel, halve, and slice them when they're cool enough to handle. Place them in a serving bowl.
6. Toss in the lime juice, orange juice, and salt to coat. Sprinkle the beets with the parsley, sage, garlic, and orange zest. The sunflower kernels and goat's cheese go on top.

Potato And Parsnip Latkes With Baked Apples

Servings: 4
Cooking Time: 20 Minutes
Ingredients:
- FOR THE LATKES
- 2 medium russet potatoes, peeled
- 1 large egg white
- 2 tablespoons all-purpose flour
- ¼ teaspoon garlic powder
- ¼ teaspoon kosher salt
- ¼ teaspoon freshly ground black pepper
- 1 medium parsnip, peeled and shredded
- 2 scallions, thinly sliced
- 2 tablespoons vegetable oil
- FOR THE BAKED APPLES
- 2 Golden Delicious apples, peeled and diced
- 2 tablespoons granulated sugar
- 2 teaspoons unsalted butter, cut into small pieces

Directions:
1. To prep the latkes: Grate the potatoes using the large holes of a box grater. Squeeze as much liquid out of the potatoes as you can into a large bowl. Set the potatoes aside in a separate bowl.
2. Let the potato liquid sit for 5 minutes, during which time the potato starch will settle to the bottom of the bowl. Pour off the water that has risen to the top, leaving the potato starch in the bowl.
3. Add the egg white, flour, salt, and black pepper to the potato starch to form a thick paste. Add the potatoes, parsnip, and scallions and mix well. Divide the mixture into 4 patties. Brush both sides of each patty with the oil.
4. To prep the baked apples: Place the apples in the Zone 2 basket. Sprinkle the sugar and butter over the top.
5. To cook the latkes and apples: Install a crisper plate in the Zone 1 basket. Place the latkes in the basket in a single layer, then insert the basket in the unit. Insert the Zone 2 basket in the unit.
6. Select Zone 1, select AIR FRY, set the temperature to 375°F, and set the timer to 15 minutes.
7. Select Zone 2, select BAKE, set the temperature to 330°F, and set the timer to 20 minutes. Select SMART FINISH.
8. Press START/PAUSE to begin cooking.
9. When both timers read 5 minutes, press START/PAUSE. Remove the Zone 1 basket and use silicone-tipped tongs or a spatula to flip the latkes. Reinsert the basket in the unit. Remove the Zone 2 basket and gently mash the apples with a fork or the back of a spoon. Reinsert the basket and press START/PAUSE to resume cooking.
10. When cooking is complete, the latkes should be golden brown and cooked through and the apples very soft.
11. Transfer the latkes to a plate and serve with apples on the side.

Nutrition:
- (Per serving) Calories: 257; Total fat: 9g; Saturated fat: 2g; Carbohydrates: 42g; Fiber: 5.5g; Protein: 4g; Sodium: 91mg

Mushroom Roll-ups

Servings: 10
Cooking Time: 10 Minutes
Ingredients:
- 2 tablespoons extra virgin olive oil
- 8 ounces large portobello mushrooms (gills discarded), finely chopped
- 1 teaspoon dried oregano
- 1 teaspoon dried thyme
- ½ teaspoon crushed red pepper flakes
- ¼ teaspoon salt
- 8 ounces cream cheese, softened
- 4 ounces whole-milk ricotta cheese
- 10 flour tortillas (8-inch)
- Cooking spray
- Chutney, for serving (optional)

Directions:
1. Heat the oil in a pan over medium heat. Add the mushrooms and cook for 4 minutes. Sauté until the mushrooms are browned, about 4-6 minutes, with the oregano, thyme, pepper flakes, and salt. Cool.
2. Combine the cheeses in a mixing bowl| fold in the mushrooms until thoroughly combined.
3. On the bottom center of each tortilla, spread 3 tablespoons of the mushroom mixture. Tightly roll up each tortilla and secure with toothpicks.
4. Place a crisper plate in each drawer. Put the roll-ups in a single layer in each. Insert the drawers into the unit.
5. Select zone 1, then AIR FRY, then set the temperature to 400 degrees F/ 200 degrees C with a 10-minute timer. To match zone 2 settings to zone 1, choose MATCH. To begin, select START/STOP.
6. Remove the roll-ups from the drawers after the timer has finished. When they have cooled enough to handle, discard the toothpicks.
7. Serve and enjoy!

Green Salad With Crispy Fried Goat Cheese And Baked Croutons

Servings: 4
Cooking Time: 10 Minutes

Ingredients:
- FOR THE GOAT CHEESE
- 1 (4-ounce) log soft goat cheese
- ½ cup panko bread crumbs
- 2 tablespoons vegetable oil
- FOR THE CROUTONS
- 2 slices Italian-style sandwich bread
- 2 tablespoons vegetable oil
- 1 tablespoon poultry seasoning
- ½ teaspoon kosher salt
- ¼ teaspoon freshly ground black pepper
- FOR THE SALAD
- 8 cups green leaf lettuce leaves
- ½ cup store-bought balsamic vinaigrette

Directions:
1. To prep the goat cheese: Cut the goat cheese into 8 round slices.
2. Spread the panko on a plate. Gently press the cheese into the panko to coat on both sides. Drizzle with the oil.
3. To prep the croutons: Cut the bread into cubes and place them in a large bowl. Add the oil, poultry seasoning, salt, and black pepper. Mix well to coat the bread cubes evenly.
4. To cook the goat cheese and croutons: Install a crisper plate in each of the two baskets. Place the goat cheese in the Zone 1 basket and insert the basket in the unit. Place the croutons in the Zone 2 basket and insert the basket in the unit.
5. Select Zone 1, select AIR FRY, set the temperature to 400°F, and set the timer to 6 minutes.
6. Select Zone 2, select BAKE, set the temperature to 390°F, and set the timer to 10 minutes. Select SMART FINISH.
7. Press START/PAUSE to begin cooking.
8. When cooking is complete, the goat cheese will be golden brown and the croutons crisp.
9. Remove the Zone 1 basket. Let the goat cheese cool in the basket for 5 minutes; it will firm up as it cools.
10. To assemble the salad: In a large bowl, combine the lettuce, vinaigrette, and croutons. Toss well. Divide the salad among four plates. Top each plate with 2 pieces of goat cheese.

Nutrition:
- (Per serving) Calories: 578; Total fat: 40g; Saturated fat: 14g; Carbohydrates: 39g; Fiber: 3.5g; Protein: 24g; Sodium: 815mg

Sweet Potatoes & Brussels Sprouts

Servings: 8
Cooking Time: 35 Minutes

Ingredients:
- 340g sweet potatoes, cubed
- 30ml olive oil
- 150g onion, cut into pieces
- 352g Brussels sprouts, halved
- Pepper
- Salt
- For glaze:
- 78ml ketchup
- 115ml balsamic vinegar
- 15g mustard
- 29 ml honey

Directions:
1. In a bowl, toss Brussels sprouts, oil, onion, sweet potatoes, pepper, and salt.
2. Insert a crisper plate in the Tefal air fryer baskets.
3. Add Brussels sprouts and sweet potato mixture in both baskets.
4. Select zone 1, then select "air fry" mode and set the temperature to 390 degrees F for 25 minutes. Press "match" to match zone 2 settings to zone 1. Press "start/stop" to begin. Stir halfway through.
5. Meanwhile, add vinegar, ketchup, honey, and mustard to a saucepan and cook over medium heat for 5-10 minutes.
6. Toss cooked sweet potatoes and Brussels sprouts with sauce.

Nutrition:
- (Per serving) Calories 142 | Fat 4.2g |Sodium 147mg | Carbs 25.2g | Fiber 4g | Sugar 8.8g | Protein 2.9g

Buffalo Seitan With Crispy Zucchini Noodles

Servings: 4
Cooking Time: 12 Minutes
Ingredients:
- FOR THE BUFFALO SEITAN
- 1 (8-ounce) package precooked seitan strips
- 1 teaspoon garlic powder, divided
- ½ teaspoon onion powder
- ¼ teaspoon smoked paprika
- ¼ cup Louisiana-style hot sauce
- 2 tablespoons vegetable oil
- 1 tablespoon tomato paste
- ¼ teaspoon freshly ground black pepper
- FOR THE ZUCCHINI NOODLES
- 3 large egg whites
- 1¼ cups all-purpose flour
- 1 teaspoon kosher salt, divided
- 12 ounces seltzer water or club soda
- 5 ounces zucchini noodles
- Nonstick cooking spray

Directions:
1. To prep the Buffalo seitan: Season the seitan strips with ½ teaspoon of garlic powder, the onion powder, and smoked paprika.
2. In a large bowl, whisk together the hot sauce, oil, tomato paste, remaining ½ teaspoon of garlic powder, and the black pepper. Set the bowl of Buffalo sauce aside.
3. To prep the zucchini noodles: In a medium bowl, use a handheld mixer to beat the egg whites until stiff peaks form.
4. In a large bowl, combine the flour and ½ teaspoon of salt. Mix in the seltzer to form a thin batter. Fold in the beaten egg whites.
5. Add the zucchini to the batter and gently mix to coat.
6. To cook the seitan and zucchini noodles: Install a crisper plate in each of the two baskets. Place the seitan in the Zone 1 basket and insert the basket in the unit. Lift the noodles from the batter one at a time, letting the excess drip off, and place them in the Zone 2 basket. Insert the basket in the unit.
7. Select Zone 1, select BAKE, set the temperature to 370°F, and set the timer to 12 minutes.
8. Select Zone 2, select AIR FRY, set the temperature to 400°F, and set the timer to 12 minutes. Select SMART FINISH.
9. Press START/PAUSE to begin cooking.
10. When the Zone 1 timer reads 2 minutes, press START/PAUSE. Remove the basket and transfer the seitan to the bowl of Buffalo sauce. Turn to coat, then return the seitan to the basket. Reinsert the basket and press START/PAUSE to resume cooking.
11. When cooking is complete, the seitan should be warmed through and the zucchini noodles crisp and light golden brown.
12. Sprinkle the zucchini noodles with the remaining ½ teaspoon of salt. If desired, drizzle extra Buffalo sauce over the seitan. Serve hot.

Nutrition:
- (Per serving) Calories: 252; Total fat: 15g; Saturated fat: 1g; Carbohydrates: 22g; Fiber: 1.5g; Protein: 13g; Sodium: 740mg

Garlic-rosemary Brussels Sprouts

Servings: 4
Cooking Time: 15 Minutes
Ingredients:
- 3 tablespoons olive oil
- 2 garlic cloves, minced
- ½ teaspoon salt
- ¼ teaspoon pepper
- 1-pound Brussels sprouts, trimmed and halved
- ½ cup panko breadcrumbs
- 1½ teaspoons minced fresh rosemary

Directions:
1. Place the first 4 ingredients in a small microwave-safe bowl| microwave on high for 30 seconds.
2. Toss the Brussels sprouts in 2 tablespoons of the microwaved mixture.
3. Place a crisper plate in each drawer. Put the sprouts in a single layer in each drawer. Insert the drawers into the units.
4. Select zone 1, then AIR FRY, then set the temperature to 360 degrees F/ 180 degrees C with a 6-minute timer. To match zone 2 settings to zone 1, choose MATCH. To begin, select START/STOP.
5. Remove the sprouts from the drawers after the timer has finished.
6. Toss the breadcrumbs with the rosemary and remaining oil mixture| sprinkle over the sprouts.
7. Continue cooking until the crumbs are browned, and the sprouts are tender . Serve immediately.

Garlic Herbed Baked Potatoes

Servings: 4
Cooking Time: 45 Minutes
Ingredients:
- 4 large baking potatoes
- Salt and black pepper, to taste
- 2 teaspoons avocado oil
- Cheese
- 2 cups sour cream
- 1 teaspoon garlic clove, minced
- 1 teaspoon fresh dill
- 2 teaspoons chopped chives
- Salt and black pepper, to taste
- 2 teaspoons Worcestershire sauce

Directions:
1. Pierce the skin of the potatoes with a fork.
2. Season the potatoes with olive oil, salt, and black pepper.
3. Divide the potatoes into the air fryer baskets.
4. Now press 1 for zone 1 and set it to AIR FRY mode at 350 degrees F/ 175 degrees C, for 45 minutes.
5. Select the MATCH button for zone 2.
6. Meanwhile, take a bowl and mix all the cheese ingredients together.
7. Once the cooking cycle is complete, take out the potatoes and make a slit in-between each one.
8. Add the cheese mixture in the cavity and serve it hot.

Jerk Tofu With Roasted Cabbage

Servings: 4
Cooking Time: 20 Minutes
Ingredients:
- FOR THE JERK TOFU
- 1 (14-ounce) package extra-firm tofu, drained
- 1 tablespoon apple cider vinegar
- 1 tablespoon reduced-sodium soy sauce
- 2 tablespoons jerk seasoning
- Juice of 1 lime
- ½ teaspoon kosher salt
- 2 tablespoons olive oil
- FOR THE CABBAGE
- 1 (14-ounce) bag coleslaw mix
- 1 red bell pepper, thinly sliced
- 2 scallions, thinly sliced
- 2 tablespoons water
- 3 garlic cloves, minced
- ¼ teaspoon fresh thyme leaves
- ¼ teaspoon onion powder
- ¼ teaspoon kosher salt
- ¼ teaspoon freshly ground black pepper

Directions:
1. To prep the jerk tofu: Cut the tofu horizontally into 4 slabs.
2. In a shallow dish (big enough to hold the tofu slabs), whisk together the vinegar, soy sauce, jerk seasoning, lime juice, and salt.
3. Place the tofu in the marinade and turn to coat both sides. Cover and marinate for at least 15 minutes (or up to overnight in the refrigerator).
4. To prep the cabbage: In the Zone 2 basket, combine the coleslaw, bell pepper, scallions, water, garlic, thyme, onion powder, salt, and black pepper.
5. To cook the tofu and cabbage: Install a crisper plate in the Zone 1 basket and add the tofu in a single layer. Brush the tofu with the oil and insert the basket in the unit. Insert the Zone 2 basket in the unit.
6. Select Zone 1, select AIR FRY, set the temperature to 390°F, and set the timer to 15 minutes.
7. Select Zone 2, select ROAST, set the temperature to 330°F, and set the timer to 20 minutes. Select SMART FINISH.
8. Press START/PAUSE to begin cooking.
9. When both timers read 5 minutes, press START/PAUSE. Remove the Zone 1 basket and use silicone-tipped tongs to flip the tofu. Reinsert the basket in the unit. Remove the Zone 2 basket and stir the cabbage. Reinsert the basket and press START/PAUSE to resume cooking.
10. When cooking is complete, the tofu will be crispy and browned around the edges and the cabbage soft.
11. Transfer the tofu to four plates and serve with the cabbage on the side.

Nutrition:
- (Per serving) Calories: 220; Total fat: 12g; Saturated fat: 1.5g; Carbohydrates: 21g; Fiber: 5g; Protein: 12g; Sodium: 817mg

Desserts Recipes

Crustless Peanut Butter Cheesecake And Pumpkin Pudding With Vanilla Wafers

Servings: 6
Cooking Time: 17 Minutes
Ingredients:
- Crustless Peanut Butter Cheesecake:
- 110 g cream cheese, softened
- 2 tablespoons powdered sweetener
- 1 tablespoon all-natural, no-sugar-added peanut butter
- ½ teaspoon vanilla extract
- 1 large egg, whisked
- Pumpkin Pudding with Vanilla Wafers:
- 250 g canned no-salt-added pumpkin purée (not pumpkin pie filling)
- 50 g packed brown sugar
- 3 tablespoons plain flour
- 1 egg, whisked
- 2 tablespoons milk
- 1 tablespoon unsalted butter, melted
- 1 teaspoon pure vanilla extract
- 4 low-fat vanilla, or plain wafers, crumbled
- Nonstick cooking spray

Directions:
1. Make the Crustless Peanut Butter Cheesecake :
2. In a medium bowl, mix cream cheese and sweetener until smooth. Add peanut butter and vanilla, mixing until smooth. Add egg and stir just until combined.
3. Spoon mixture into an ungreased springform pan and place into the zone 1 air fryer drawer. Adjust the temperature to 148°C and bake for 10 minutes. Edges will be firm, but center will be mostly set with only a small amount of jiggle when done.
4. Let pan cool at room temperature 30 minutes, cover with plastic wrap, then place into refrigerator at least 2 hours. Serve chilled.
5. Make the Pumpkin Pudding with Vanilla Wafers :
6. Preheat the air fryer to 176°C. Coat a baking pan with nonstick cooking spray. Set aside.
7. Mix the pumpkin purée, brown sugar, flour, whisked egg, milk, melted butter, and vanilla in a medium bowl and whisk to combine. Transfer the mixture to the baking pan.
8. Place the baking pan in the zone 2 air fryer drawer and bake for 12 to 17 minutes until set.
9. Remove the pudding from the drawer to a wire rack to cool.
10. Divide the pudding into four bowls and serve with the vanilla wafers sprinkled on top.

Apple Nutmeg Flautas

Servings: 8
Cooking Time: 8 Minutes.
Ingredients:
- ¼ cup light brown sugar
- ⅛ cup all-purpose flour
- ¼ teaspoon ground cinnamon
- Nutmeg, to taste
- 4 apples, peeled, cored & sliced
- ½ lemon, juice, and zest
- 6 (10-inch) flour tortillas
- Vegetable oil
- Caramel sauce
- Cinnamon sugar

Directions:
1. Mix brown sugar with cinnamon, nutmeg, and flour in a large bowl.
2. Toss in apples in lemon juice. Mix well.
3. Place a tortilla at a time on a flat surface and add ½ cup of the apple mixture to the tortilla.
4. Roll the tortilla into a burrito and seal it tightly and hold it in place with a toothpick.
5. Repeat the same steps with the remaining tortillas and apple mixture.
6. Place two apple burritos in each of the crisper plate and spray them with cooking oil.
7. Return the crisper plates to the Tefal Dual Zone Air Fryer.
8. Choose the Air Fry mode for Zone 1 and set the temperature to 400 degrees F and the time to 8 minutes.
9. Select the "MATCH" button to copy the settings for Zone 2.
10. Initiate cooking by pressing the START/STOP button.
11. Flip the burritos once cooked halfway through, then resume cooking.
12. Garnish with caramel sauce and cinnamon sugar.
13. Enjoy!

Nutrition:
- (Per serving) Calories 157 | Fat 1.3g | Sodium 27mg | Carbs 1.3g | Fiber 1g | Sugar 2.2g | Protein 8.2g

Apple Fritters

Servings: 14
Cooking Time: 10 Minutes
Ingredients:
- 2 large apples
- 2 cups all-purpose flour
- ½ cup granulated sugar
- 1 tablespoon baking powder
- 1 teaspoon salt
- 1 teaspoon ground cinnamon
- ½ teaspoon ground nutmeg
- ¼ teaspoon ground cloves
- ¾ cup apple cider or apple juice
- 2 eggs
- 3 tablespoons butter, melted
- 1 teaspoon vanilla extract
- For the apple cider glaze:
- 2 cups powdered sugar
- ¼ cup apple cider or apple juice
- ½ teaspoon ground cinnamon
- ¼ teaspoon ground nutmeg

Directions:
1. Peel and core the apples, then cut them into ¼-inch cubes. Spread the apple chunks out on a kitchen towel to absorb any excess moisture.
2. In a mixing bowl, combine the flour, sugar, baking powder, salt, and spices.
3. Add the apple chunks and combine well.
4. Whisk together the apple cider, eggs, melted butter, and vanilla in a small bowl.
5. Combine the wet and dry in a large mixing bowl.
6. Install a crisper plate in both drawers. Use an ice cream scoop to scoop 3 to 4 dollops of fritter dough into the zone 1 drawer and 3 to 4 dollops into the zone 2 drawer. Insert the drawers into the unit. You may need to cook in batches.
7. Select zone 1, select BAKE, set temperature to 390°F, and set time to 10 minutes. Select MATCH to match zone 2 settings to zone 1. Press the START/STOP button to begin cooking.
8. Meanwhile, make the glaze: Whisk the powdered sugar, apple cider, and spices together until smooth.
9. When the fritters are cooked, drizzle the glaze over them. Let sit for 10 minutes until the glaze sets.

Delicious Apple Fritters

Servings: 10
Cooking Time: 8 Minutes
Ingredients:
- 236g Bisquick
- 2 apples, peel & dice
- 158ml milk
- 30ml butter, melted
- 1 tsp cinnamon
- 24g sugar

Directions:
1. In a bowl, mix Bisquick, cinnamon, and sugar.
2. Add milk and mix until dough forms. Add apple and stir well.
3. Insert a crisper plate in Tefal air fryer baskets.
4. Make fritters from the mixture and place in both baskets. Brush fritters with melted butter.
5. Select zone 1 then select "air fry" mode and set the temperature to 360 degrees F for 10 minutes. Press "match" to match zone 2 settings to zone 1. Press "start/stop" to begin.

Nutrition:
- (Per serving) Calories 171 | Fat 6.7g | Sodium 352mg | Carbs 25.8g | Fiber 1.7g | Sugar 10.8g | Protein 2.7g

Fried Oreos

Servings: 8
Cooking Time: 8 Minutes
Ingredients:
- 1 can Pillsbury Crescent Dough (or equivalent)
- 8 Oreo cookies
- 1–2 tablespoons powdered sugar

Directions:
1. Open the crescent dough up and cut it into the right-size pieces to completely wrap each cookie.
2. Wrap each Oreo in dough. Make sure that there are no air bubbles and that the cookies are completely covered.
3. Install a crisper plate in both drawers. Place half the Oreo cookies in the zone 1 drawer and half in zone 2's. Sprinkle the tops with the powdered sugar, then insert the drawers into the unit.
4. Select zone 1, select AIR FRY, set temperature to 390°F, and set time to 8 minutes. Select MATCH to match zone 2 settings to zone 1. Press the START/STOP button to begin cooking.
5. Serve warm and enjoy!

Banana Spring Rolls With Hot Fudge Dip

Servings: 4
Cooking Time: 10 Minutes

Ingredients:
- FOR THE BANANA SPRING ROLLS
- 1 large banana
- 4 egg roll wrappers
- 4 teaspoons light brown sugar
- Nonstick cooking spray
- FOR THE HOT FUDGE DIP
- ¼ cup sweetened condensed milk
- 2 tablespoons semisweet chocolate chips
- 1 tablespoon unsweetened cocoa powder
- 1 tablespoon unsalted butter
- ⅛ teaspoon kosher salt
- ⅛ teaspoon vanilla extract

Directions:
1. To prep the banana spring rolls: Peel the banana and halve it crosswise. Cut each piece in half lengthwise, for a total of 4 pieces.
2. Place one piece of banana diagonally across an egg roll wrapper. Sprinkle with 1 teaspoon of brown sugar. Fold the edges of the egg roll wrapper over the ends of the banana, then roll to enclose the banana inside. Brush the edge of the wrapper with water and press to seal. Spritz with cooking spray. Repeat with the remaining bananas, egg roll wrappers, and brown sugar.
3. To prep the hot fudge dip: In an ovenproof ramekin or bowl, combine the condensed milk, chocolate chips, cocoa powder, butter, salt, and vanilla.
4. To cook the spring rolls and hot fudge dip: Install a crisper plate in each of the two baskets. Place the banana spring rolls seam-side down in the Zone 1 basket and insert the basket in the unit. Place the ramekin in the Zone 2 basket and insert the basket in the unit.
5. Select Zone 1, select AIR FRY, set the temperature to 390°F, and set the timer to 10 minutes.
6. Select Zone 2, select BAKE, set the temperature to 330°F, and set the timer to 8 minutes. Select SMART FINISH.
7. Press START/PAUSE to begin cooking.
8. When the Zone 2 timer reads 3 minutes, press START/PAUSE. Remove the basket and stir the hot fudge until smooth. Reinsert the basket and press START/PAUSE to resume cooking.
9. When cooking is complete, the spring rolls should be crisp.
10. Let the hot fudge cool for 2 to 3 minutes. Serve the banana spring rolls with hot fudge for dipping.

Nutrition:
- (Per serving) Calories: 268; Total fat: 10g; Saturated fat: 4g; Carbohydrates: 42g; Fiber: 2g; Protein: 5g; Sodium: 245mg

Simple Pineapple Sticks And Crispy Pineapple Rings

Servings: 9
Cooking Time: 10 Minutes

Ingredients:
- Simple Pineapple Sticks:
- ½ fresh pineapple, cut into sticks
- 25 g desiccated coconut
- Crispy Pineapple Rings:
- 240 ml rice milk
- 85 g plain flour
- 120 ml water
- 25 g unsweetened flaked coconut
- 4 tablespoons granulated sugar
- ½ teaspoon baking soda
- ½ teaspoon baking powder
- ½ teaspoon vanilla essence
- ½ teaspoon ground cinnamon
- ¼ teaspoon ground star anise
- Pinch of kosher, or coarse sea salt
- 1 medium pineapple, peeled and sliced

Directions:
1. Simple Pineapple Sticks :
2. Preheat the air fryer to 204°C.
3. Coat the pineapple sticks in the desiccated coconut and put in the zone 1 air fryer drawer.
4. Air fry for 10 minutes.
5. Serve immediately
6. Crispy Pineapple Rings :
7. Preheat the air fryer to 204°C.
8. In a large bowl, stir together all the ingredients except the pineapple.
9. Dip each pineapple slice into the batter until evenly coated.
10. Arrange the pineapple slices in the zone 2 drawer and air fry for 6 to 8 minutes until golden brown.
11. Remove from the drawer to a plate and cool for 5 minutes before serving warm

Easy Mini Chocolate Chip Pan Cookie

Servings: 4
Cooking Time: 7 Minutes
Ingredients:
- ½ cup blanched finely ground almond flour
- ¼ cup powdered erythritol
- 2 tablespoons unsalted butter, softened
- 1 large egg
- ½ teaspoon unflavored gelatin
- ½ teaspoon baking powder
- ½ teaspoon vanilla extract
- 2 tablespoons low-carb, sugar-free chocolate chips

Directions:
1. Combine erythritol and almond flour in a large bowl. Add in egg, gelatin, and butter , stir well.
2. Stir in vanilla and baking powder and then fold in chocolate chips. Spoon batter into 6&quot| round baking pan. Put pan into the air fryer basket.
3. Set the temperature to 300°F, then set the timer for 7 minutes.
4. The top of the cookie will be golden brown and a toothpick inserted in center will come out clean when fully cooked. Allow to rest for more than 10 minutes.

Coconut-custard Pie And Pecan Brownies

Servings: 9
Cooking Time: 20 To 23 Minutes
Ingredients:
- Coconut-Custard Pie:
- 240 ml milk
- 50 g granulated sugar, plus 2 tablespoons
- 30 g scone mix
- 1 teaspoon vanilla extract
- 2 eggs
- 2 tablespoons melted butter
- Cooking spray
- 50 g desiccated, sweetened coconut
- Pecan Brownies:
- 50 g blanched finely ground almond flour
- 55 g powdered sweetener
- 2 tablespoons unsweetened cocoa powder
- ½ teaspoon baking powder
- 55 g unsalted butter, softened
- 1 large egg
- 35 g chopped pecans
- 40 g low-carb, sugar-free chocolate chips

Directions:
1. Make the Coconut-Custard Pie :
2. Place all ingredients except coconut in a medium bowl.
3. Using a hand mixer, beat on high speed for 3 minutes.
4. Let sit for 5 minutes.
5. Preheat the air fryer to 164ºC.
6. Spray a baking pan with cooking spray and place pan in the zone 1 air fryer drawer.
7. Pour filling into pan and sprinkle coconut over top.
8. Cook pie for 20 to 23 minutes or until center sets.
9. Make the Pecan Brownies :
10. In a large bowl, mix almond flour, sweetener, cocoa powder, and baking powder. Stir in butter and egg. 2. Fold in pecans and chocolate chips. Scoop mixture into a round baking pan. Place pan into the zone 2 air fryer drawer. 3. Adjust the temperature to 148ºC and bake for 20 minutes. 4. When fully cooked a toothpick inserted in center will come out clean. Allow 20 minutes to fully cool and firm up.

Air Fried Bananas

Servings: 4
Cooking Time: 15 Minutes
Ingredients:
- 4 bananas, sliced
- 1 avocado oil cooking spray

Directions:
1. Spread the banana slices in the two crisper plates in a single layer.
2. Drizzle avocado oil over the banana slices.
3. Return the crisper plate to the Tefal Dual Zone Air Fryer.
4. Choose the Air Fry mode for Zone 1 and set the temperature to 350 degrees F and the time to 13 minutes.
5. Select the "MATCH" button to copy the settings for Zone 2.
6. Initiate cooking by pressing the START/STOP button.
7. Serve.

Chocolate Mug Cakes

Servings: 4
Cooking Time: 20 Minutes
Ingredients:
- 1 cup flour
- 8 tablespoons sugar
- 1 teaspoon baking powder
- ½ teaspoon baking soda
- ¼ teaspoon salt
- 8 tablespoons milk
- 8 tablespoons applesauce
- 2 tablespoons vegetable oil
- 1 teaspoon vanilla extract
- 8 tablespoons chocolate chips

Directions:
1. Press "Zone 1" and "Zone 2" and then rotate the knob for each zone to select "Bake".
2. Set the temperature to 375 degrees F/ 190 degrees C for both zones and then set the time for 5 minutes to preheat.
3. In a bowl, mix together the flour, sugar, baking powder, baking soda and salt.
4. Add the milk, applesauce, oil and vanilla extract and mix until well combined.
5. Gently fold in the chocolate chips.
6. Divide the mixture into 4 heatproof mugs.
7. After preheating, arrange 2 mugs into the basket of each zone.
8. Slide each basket into Air Fryer and set the time for 17 minutes.
9. After cooking time is completed, remove the mugs from Air Fryer.
10. Place the mugs onto a wire rack to cool for about 10 minutes before serving.

Mini Peanut Butter Tarts

Servings: 8
Cooking Time: 12 To 15 Minutes
Ingredients:
- 125 g pecans
- 110 g finely ground blanched almond flour
- 2 tablespoons unsalted butter, at room temperature
- 50 g powdered sweetener, plus 2 tablespoons, divided
- 120 g heavy (whipping) cream
- 2 tablespoons mascarpone cheese
- 110 g cream cheese
- 140 g sugar-free peanut butter
- 1 teaspoon pure vanilla extract
- ⅛ teaspoon sea salt
- 85 g organic chocolate chips
- 1 tablespoon coconut oil
- 40 g chopped peanuts or pecans

Directions:
1. Place the pecans in the bowl of a food processor; process until they are finely ground.
2. Transfer the ground pecans to a medium bowl and stir in the almond flour. Add the butter and 2 tablespoons of sweetener and stir until the mixture becomes wet and crumbly.
3. Divide the mixture among 8 silicone muffin cups, pressing the crust firmly with your fingers into the bottom and part way up the sides of each cup.
4. Arrange the muffin cups in the two air fryer drawers. Set the air fryer to 148°C and bake for 12 to 15 minutes, until the crusts begin to brown. Remove the cups from the air fryer and set them aside to cool.
5. In the bowl of a stand mixer, combine the heavy cream and mascarpone cheese. Beat until peaks form. Transfer to a large bowl.
6. In the same stand mixer bowl, combine the cream cheese, peanut butter, remaining 50 g sweetener, vanilla, and salt. Beat at medium-high speed until smooth.
7. Reduce the speed to low and add the heavy cream mixture back a spoonful at a time, beating after each addition.
8. Spoon the peanut butter mixture over the crusts and freeze the tarts for 30 minutes.
9. Place the chocolate chips and coconut oil in the top of a double boiler over high heat. Stir until melted, then remove from the heat.
10. Drizzle the melted chocolate over the peanut butter tarts. Top with the chopped nuts and freeze the tarts for another 15 minutes, until set.
11. Store the peanut butter tarts in an airtight container in the refrigerator for up to 1 week or in the freezer for up to 1 month.

Air Fried Beignets

Servings: 6
Cooking Time: 17 Minutes.
Ingredients:
- Cooking spray
- ¼ cup white sugar
- ⅛ cup water
- ½ cup all-purpose flour
- 1 large egg, separated
- 1 ½ teaspoons butter, melted
- ½ teaspoon baking powder
- ½ teaspoon vanilla extract
- 1 pinch salt
- 2 tablespoons confectioners' sugar, or to taste

Directions:
1. Beat flour with water, sugar, egg yolk, baking powder, butter, vanilla extract, and salt in a large bowl until lumps-free.
2. Beat egg whites in a separate bowl and beat using an electric hand mixer until it forms soft peaks.
3. Add the egg white to the flour batter and mix gently until fully incorporated.
4. Divide the dough into small beignets and place them in the crisper plate.
5. Return the crisper plate to the Tefal Dual Zone Air Fryer.
6. Choose the Air Fry mode for Zone 1 and set the temperature to 390 degrees F and the time to 17 minutes.
7. Select the "MATCH" button to copy the settings for Zone 2.
8. Initiate cooking by pressing the START/STOP button.
9. And cook for another 4 minutes. Dust the cooked beignets with sugar.
10. Serve.

Nutrition:
- (Per serving) Calories 327 | Fat 14.2g |Sodium 672mg | Carbs 47.2g | Fiber 1.7g | Sugar 24.8g | Protein 4.4g

S'mores Dip With Cinnamon-sugar Tortillas

Servings: 4
Cooking Time: 5 Minutes
Ingredients:
- FOR THE S'MORES DIP
- ½ cup chocolate-hazelnut spread
- ¼ cup milk chocolate or white chocolate chips
- ¼ cup graham cracker crumbs
- ½ cup mini marshmallows
- FOR THE CINNAMON-SUGAR TORTILLAS
- 4 (6-inch) flour tortillas
- Butter-flavored cooking spray
- 1 teaspoon granulated sugar
- ½ teaspoon ground cinnamon
- ¼ teaspoon ground cardamom (optional)

Directions:
1. To prep the s'mores dip: Spread the chocolate-hazelnut spread in the bottom of a shallow ovenproof ramekin or dish.
2. Scatter the chocolate chips and graham cracker crumbs over the top. Arrange the marshmallows in a single layer on top of the crumbs.
3. To prep the tortillas: Spray both sides of each tortilla with cooking spray. Cut each tortilla into 8 wedges and sprinkle both sides evenly with sugar, cinnamon, and cardamom (if using).
4. To cook the dip and tortillas: Install a crisper plate in each of the two baskets. Place the ramekin in the Zone 1 basket and insert the basket in the unit. Place the tortillas in the Zone 2 basket and insert the basket in the unit.
5. Select Zone 1, select BAKE, set the temperature to 330°F, and set the timer to 5 minutes.
6. Select Zone 2, select AIR FRY, set the temperature to 375°F, and set the timer to 5 minutes. Select SMART FINISH.
7. Press START/PAUSE to begin cooking.
8. When the Zone 2 timer reads 3 minutes, press START/PAUSE. Remove the basket and shake it to redistribute the chips. Reinsert the basket and press START/PAUSE to resume cooking.
9. When cooking is complete, the dip will be bubbling and golden brown and the chips crispy.
10. If desired, toast the marshmallows more: Select Zone 1, select AIR BROIL, set the temperature to 450°F, and set the timer to 1 minute. Cook until the marshmallows are deep golden brown.
11. Let the dip cool for 2 to 3 minutes. Serve with the cinnamon-sugar tortilla chips.

Nutrition:
- (Per serving) Calories: 404; Total fat: 18g; Saturated fat: 7g; Carbohydrates: 54g; Fiber: 2.5g; Protein: 6g; Sodium: 346mg

Pumpkin-spice Bread Pudding

Servings: 6
Cooking Time: 35 Minutes
Ingredients:
- Bread Pudding:
- 175 ml heavy whipping cream
- 120 g canned pumpkin
- 80 ml whole milk
- 65 g granulated sugar
- 1 large egg plus 1 yolk
- ½ teaspoon pumpkin pie spice
- ⅛ teaspoon kosher, or coarse sea salt
- 1/3 loaf of day-old baguette or crusty country bread, cubed
- 4 tablespoons unsalted butter, melted
- Sauce:
- 80 ml pure maple syrup
- 1 tablespoon unsalted butter
- 120 ml heavy whipping cream
- ½ teaspoon pure vanilla extract

Directions:
1. For the bread pudding: In a medium bowl, combine the cream, pumpkin, milk, sugar, egg and yolk, pumpkin pie spice, and salt. Whisk until well combined. 2. In a large bowl, toss the bread cubes with the melted butter. Add the pumpkin mixture and gently toss until the ingredients are well combined. 3. Transfer the mixture to a baking pan. Place the pan in the zone 1 air fryer drawer. Set the temperature to 176°C cooking for 35 minutes, or until custard is set in the middle. 4. Meanwhile, for the sauce: In a small saucepan, combine the syrup and butter. Heat over medium heat, stirring, until the butter melts. Stir in the cream and simmer, stirring often, until the sauce has thickened, about 15 minutes. Stir in the vanilla. Remove the pudding from the air fryer. 5. Let the pudding stand for 10 minutes before serving with the warm sauce.

Maple-pecan Tart With Sea Salt

Servings: 8
Cooking Time: 25 Minutes
Ingredients:
- Tart Crust:
- Vegetable oil spray
- 75 g unsalted butter, softened
- 50 g firmly packed brown sugar
- 125 g plain flour
- ¼ teaspoon kosher, or coarse sea salt
- Filling:
- 4 tablespoons unsalted butter, diced
- 95 g packed brown sugar
- 60 ml pure maple syrup
- 60 ml whole milk
- ¼ teaspoon pure vanilla extract
- 190 g finely chopped pecans
- ¼ teaspoon flaked sea salt

Directions:
1. For the crust: Line a baking pan with foil, leaving a couple of inches of overhang. Spray the foil with vegetable oil spray. 2. In a medium bowl, combine the butter and brown sugar. Beat with an electric mixer on medium-low speed until light and fluffy. Add the flour and kosher salt and beat until the ingredients are well blended. Transfer the mixture to the prepared pan. Press it evenly into the bottom of the pan. 3. Place the pan in the zone 1 air fryer drawer. Set the temperature to 176°C and cook for 13 minutes. When the crust has 5 minutes left to cook, start the filling. 4. For the filling: In a medium saucepan, combine the butter, brown sugar, maple syrup, and milk. Bring to a simmer, stirring occasionally. When it begins simmering, cook for 1 minute. Remove from the heat and stir in the vanilla and pecans. 5. Carefully pour the filling evenly over the crust, gently spreading with a rubber spatula so the nuts and liquid are evenly distributed. Keep the air fryer at 176°C and cook for 12 minutes, or until mixture is bubbling. 6. Remove the pan from the air fryer and sprinkle the tart with the sea salt. Cool completely on a wire rack until room temperature. 7. Transfer the pan to the refrigerator to chill. When cold, use the foil overhang to remove the tart from the pan and cut into 8 wedges. Serve at room temperature.

Simple Cheesecake

Servings: 3
Cooking Time: 20 Minutes
Ingredients:
- ½ egg
- 2 tablespoons sugar
- ⅛ teaspoon vanilla extract
- ¼ cup honey graham cracker crumbs
- ½ tablespoon unsalted butter, softened
- ¼ pound cream cheese, softened

Directions:
1. Line a round baking dish with parchment paper.
2. For crust: In a bowl, add the graham cracker crumbs and butter.
3. Place the crust into baking dish and press to smooth.
4. Press "Zone 1" and "Zone 2" and then rotate the knob for each zone to select "Bake".
5. Set the temperature to 350 degrees F/ 175 degrees C for both zones and then set the time for 5 minutes to preheat.
6. After preheating, arrange the baking dish into the basket of each zone.
7. Slide each basket into Air Fryer and set the time for 4 minutes.
8. Remove the crust from the oven and set aside to cool slightly.
9. Meanwhile, take a bowl, add the cream cheese and sugar. Whisk until smooth.
10. Now, place the eggs, one at a time and whisk until mixture becomes creamy.
11. Add the vanilla extract and mix well.
12. Place the cream cheese mixture evenly over the crust.
13. Arrange the baking dish into the Air-Fryer basket.
14. Remove from the oven and set aside to cool.
15. Serve and enjoy!

Pumpkin Hand Pies Blueberry Hand Pies

Servings: 4
Cooking Time: 15 Minutes
Ingredients:
- FOR THE PUMPKIN HAND PIES
- ½ cup pumpkin pie filling (from a 15-ounce can)
- ⅓ cup half-and-half
- 1 large egg
- ½ refrigerated pie crust (from a 14.1-ounce package)
- 1 large egg yolk
- 1 tablespoon whole milk
- FOR THE BLUEBERRY HAND PIES
- ¼ cup blueberries
- 2 tablespoons granulated sugar
- 1 tablespoon grated lemon zest (optional)
- ¼ teaspoon cornstarch
- 1 teaspoon fresh lemon juice
- ⅛ teaspoon kosher salt
- ½ refrigerated pie crust (from a 14.1-ounce package)
- 1 large egg yolk
- 1 tablespoon whole milk
- ½ teaspoon turbinado sugar

Directions:
1. To prep the pumpkin hand pies: In a small bowl, mix the pumpkin pie filling, half-and-half, and whole egg until well combined and smooth.
2. Cut the dough in half to form two wedges. Divide the pumpkin pie filling between the wedges. Fold the crust over to completely encase the filling. Using a fork, crimp the edges, forming a tight seal.
3. In a small bowl, whisk together the egg yolk and milk. Brush over the pastry. Carefully cut two small vents in the top of each pie.
4. To prep the blueberry hand pies: In a small bowl, combine the blueberries, granulated sugar, lemon zest (if using), cornstarch, lemon juice, and salt.
5. Cut the dough in half to form two wedges. Divide the blueberry filling between the wedges. Fold the crust over to completely encase the filling. Using a fork, crimp the edges, forming a tight seal.
6. In a small bowl, whisk together the egg yolk and milk. Brush over the pastry. Sprinkle with the turbinado sugar. Carefully cut two small vents in the top of each pie.
7. To cook the hand pies: Install a crisper plate in each of the two baskets. Place the pumpkin hand pies in the Zone 1 basket and insert the basket in the unit. Place the blueberry hand pies in the Zone 2 basket and insert the basket in the unit.
8. Select Zone 1, select AIR FRY, set the temperature to 350°F, and set the timer to 15 minutes. Select MATCH COOK to match Zone 2 settings to Zone 1.
9. Press START/PAUSE to begin cooking.
10. When cooking is complete, the pie crust should be crisp and golden brown and the filling bubbling.
11. Let the hand pies cool for at least 30 minutes before serving.

Nutrition:
- (Per serving) Calories: 588; Total fat: 33g; Saturated fat: 14g; Carbohydrates: 68g; Fiber: 0.5g; Protein: 10g; Sodium: 583mg

Bread Pudding

Servings: 2
Cooking Time: 15 Minutes
Ingredients:
- Nonstick spray, for greasing ramekins
- 2 slices of white bread, crumbled
- 4 tablespoons white sugar
- 5 large eggs
- ½ cup cream
- Salt, pinch
- ⅓ teaspoon cinnamon powder

Directions:
1. Take a bowl and whisk eggs in it.
2. Add sugar and salt to the eggs and whisk it all well.
3. Then add cream and use a hand beater to incorporate the Ingredients:.
4. Next add cinnamon, and the crumbled white bread.
5. Mix it well and add into two round shaped baking pans.
6. Place each baking pan in the air fryer basket.
7. Set zone 1 to AIR FRY mode at 350 degrees F for 8-12 minutes.
8. Press MATCH button for zone 2.
9. Once it's cooked, serve.

Gluten-free Spice Cookies

Servings: 4
Cooking Time: 12 Minutes
Ingredients:
- 4 tablespoons unsalted butter, at room temperature
- 2 tablespoons agave nectar
- 1 large egg
- 2 tablespoons water
- 240 g almond flour
- 100 g granulated sugar
- 2 teaspoons ground ginger
- 1 teaspoon ground cinnamon
- ½ teaspoon freshly grated nutmeg
- 1 teaspoon baking soda
- ¼ teaspoon kosher, or coarse sea salt

Directions:
1. Line the bottom of the air fryer basket with baking paper cut to fit.
2. In a large bowl, using a hand mixer, beat together the butter, agave, egg, and water on medium speed until light and fluffy.
3. Add the almond flour, sugar, ginger, cinnamon, nutmeg, baking soda, and salt. Beat on low speed until well combined.
4. Roll the dough into 2-tablespoon balls and arrange them on the baking paper in the basket. Set the air fryer to 165°C, and cook for 12 minutes, or until the tops of cookies are lightly browned.
5. Transfer to a wire rack and let cool completely. Store in an airtight container for up to a week.

Pecan Brownies And Cinnamon-sugar Almonds

Servings: 10
Cooking Time: 20 Minutes
Ingredients:
- Pecan Brownies:
- 50 g blanched finely ground almond flour
- 55 g powdered sweetener
- 2 tablespoons unsweetened cocoa powder
- ½ teaspoon baking powder
- 55 g unsalted butter, softened
- 1 large egg
- 35 g chopped pecans
- 40 g low-carb, sugar-free chocolate chips
- Cinnamon-Sugar Almonds:
- 150 g whole almonds
- 2 tablespoons salted butter, melted
- 1 tablespoon granulated sugar
- ½ teaspoon ground cinnamon

Directions:
1. Make the Pecan Brownies :
2. In a large bowl, mix almond flour, sweetener, cocoa powder, and baking powder. Stir in butter and egg.
3. Fold in pecans and chocolate chips. Scoop mixture into a round baking pan. Place pan into the zone 1 air fryer basket.
4. Adjust the temperature to 150°C and bake for 20 minutes.
5. When fully cooked a toothpick inserted in center will come out clean. Allow 20 minutes to fully cool and firm up.
6. Make the Cinnamon-Sugar Almonds :
7. In a medium bowl, combine the almonds, butter, sugar, and cinnamon. Mix well to ensure all the almonds are coated with the spiced butter.
8. Transfer the almonds to the zone 2 air fryer basket and shake so they are in a single layer. Set the air fryer to 150°C, and cook for 8 minutes, stirring the almonds halfway through the cooking time.
9. Let cool completely before serving.

Cinnamon Sugar Dessert Fries

Servings: 4
Cooking Time: 15 Minutes
Ingredients:
- 2 sweet potatoes
- 1 tablespoon butter, melted
- 1 teaspoon butter, melted
- 2 tablespoons sugar
- ½ teaspoon ground cinnamon

Directions:
1. Peel and cut the sweet potatoes into skinny fries.
2. Coat the fries with 1 tablespoon of butter.
3. Install a crisper plate into each drawer. Place half the sweet potatoes in the zone 1 drawer and half in zone 2's, then insert the drawers into the unit.
4. Select zone 1, select AIR FRY, set temperature to 390°F, and set time to 15 minutes. Select MATCH to match zone 2 settings to zone 1. Press the START/STOP button to begin cooking.
5. When the time reaches 11 minutes, press START/STOP to pause the unit. Remove the drawers and flip the fries. Re-insert the drawers into the unit and press START/STOP to resume cooking.
6. Meanwhile, mix the 1 teaspoon of butter, the sugar, and the cinnamon in a large bowl.
7. When the fries are done, add them to the bowl, and toss them to coat.
8. Serve and enjoy!

Berry Crumble And S'mores

Servings: 8
Cooking Time: 15 Minutes
Ingredients:
- Berry Crumble:
- For the Filling:
- 300 g mixed berries
- 2 tablespoons sugar
- 1 tablespoon cornflour
- 1 tablespoon fresh lemon juice
- For the Topping:
- 30 g plain flour
- 20 g rolled oats
- 1 tablespoon granulated sugar
- 2 tablespoons cold unsalted butter, cut into small cubes
- Whipped cream or ice cream (optional)
- S'mores:
- Coconut, or avocado oil, for spraying
- 8 digestive biscuits
- 2 (45 g) chocolate bars
- 4 large marshmallows

Directions:
1. Make the Berry Crumble :
2. 1. Preheat the air fryer to 204°C. For the filling: In a round baking pan, gently mix the berries, sugar, cornflour, and lemon juice until thoroughly combined.
3. For the topping: In a small bowl, combine the flour, oats, and sugar. Stir the butter into the flour mixture until the mixture has the consistency of breadcrumbs.
4. Sprinkle the topping over the berries. 5. Put the pan in the zone 1 air fryer drawer and air fry for 15 minutes. Let cool for 5 minutes on a wire rack. 6. Serve topped with whipped cream or ice cream, if desired.
3. Make the S'mores :
4. Line the zone 2 air fryer drawer with baking paper and spray lightly with oil.
5. Place 4 biscuits into the prepared drawer.
6. Break the chocolate bars in half, and place 1/2 on top of each biscuit. Top with 1 marshmallow.
7. Air fry at 188°C for 30 seconds, or until the marshmallows are puffed, golden brown and slightly melted.
8. Top with the remaining biscuits and serve.

Cream Cheese Shortbread Cookies

Servings: 12 Cookies
Cooking Time: 20 Minutes
Ingredients:
- 60 ml coconut oil, melted
- 55 g cream cheese, softened
- 100 g granulated sweetener
- 1 large egg, whisked
- 190 g blanched finely ground almond flour
- 1 teaspoon almond extract

Directions:
1. Combine all ingredients in a large bowl to form a firm ball.
2. Place dough on a sheet of plastic wrap and roll into a 12-inch-long log shape. Roll log in plastic wrap and place in refrigerator 30 minutes to chill.
3. Remove log from plastic and slice into twelve equal cookies. Cut two sheets of baking paper to fit the two air fryer baskets. Place the cookies on the two ungreased sheet and put into the two air fryer baskets. Adjust the temperature to 160°C and bake for 10 minutes, turning cookies halfway through cooking. They will be lightly golden when done.
4. Let cool 15 minutes before serving to avoid crumbling.

Peanut Butter, Honey & Banana Toast

Servings: 4
Cooking Time: 9 Minutes
Ingredients:
- 2 tablespoons unsalted butter, softened
- 4 slices white bread
- 4 tablespoons peanut butter
- 2 bananas, peeled and thinly sliced
- 4 tablespoons honey
- 1 teaspoon ground cinnamon

Directions:
1. Spread butter on one side of each slice of bread, then peanut butter on the other side. Arrange the banana slices on top of the peanut butter sides of each slice. Drizzle honey on top of the banana and sprinkle with cinnamon.
2. Cut each slice in half lengthwise so that it will better fit into the air fryer basket. Arrange the bread slices, butter sides down, in the two air fryer baskets. Set the air fryer to 190°C cooking for 5 minutes. Then set the air fryer to 205°C and cook for an additional 4 minutes, or until the bananas have started to brown. Serve hot.

Grilled Peaches

Servings: 4
Cooking Time: 10 Minutes
Ingredients:
- 2 yellow peaches
- ¼ cup graham cracker crumbs
- ¼ cup brown sugar
- ¼ cup butter, diced into tiny cubes
- Whipped cream or ice cream, for serving.

Directions:
1. Cut the peaches into wedges and pull out their pits.
2. Install a crisper plate in both drawers. Put half of the peach wedges into the drawer in zone 1 and half in zone 2's. Sprinkle the tops of the wedges with the crumbs, sugar, and butter. Insert the drawers into the unit.
3. Select zone 1, select AIR FRY, set the temperature to 390°F, and set the time to 10 minutes. Select MATCH to match zone 2 settings to zone 1. Press the START/STOP button to begin cooking.

Walnut Baklava Bites Pistachio Baklava Bites

Servings: 12
Cooking Time: 10 Minutes
Ingredients:
- FOR THE WALNUT BAKLAVA BITES
- ¼ cup finely chopped walnuts
- 2 teaspoons cold unsalted butter, grated
- 2 teaspoons granulated sugar
- ½ teaspoon ground cinnamon
- 6 frozen phyllo shells (from a 1.9-ounce package), thawed
- FOR THE PISTACHIO BAKLAVA BITES
- ¼ cup finely chopped pistachios
- 2 teaspoons very cold unsalted butter, grated
- 2 teaspoons granulated sugar
- ¼ teaspoon ground cardamom (optional)
- 6 frozen phyllo shells (from a 1.9-ounce package), thawed
- FOR THE HONEY SYRUP
- ¼ cup hot water
- ¼ cup honey
- 2 teaspoons fresh lemon juice

Directions:
1. To prep the walnut baklava bites: In a small bowl, combine the walnuts, butter, sugar, and cinnamon. Spoon the filling into the phyllo shells.
2. To prep the pistachio baklava bites: In a small bowl, combine the pistachios, butter, sugar, and cardamom (if using). Spoon the filling into the phyllo shells.
3. To cook the baklava bites: Install a crisper plate in each of the two baskets. Place the walnut baklava bites in the Zone 1 basket and insert the basket in the unit. Place the pistachio baklava bites in the Zone 2 basket and insert the basket in the unit.
4. Select Zone 1, select BAKE, set the temperature to 330°F, and set the timer to 10 minutes. Press MATCH COOK to match Zone 2 settings to Zone 1.
5. Press START/PAUSE to begin cooking.
6. When cooking is complete, the shells will be golden brown and crisp.
7. To make the honey syrup: In a small bowl, whisk together the hot water, honey, and lemon juice. Dividing evenly, pour the syrup over the baklava bites (you may hear a crackling sound).
8. Let cool completely before serving, about 1 hour.

Nutrition:
- (Per serving) Calories: 262; Total fat: 16g; Saturated fat: 3g; Carbohydrates: 29g; Fiber: 1g; Protein: 2g; Sodium: 39mg

Cinnamon Bread Twists

Servings: 4
Cooking Time: 15 Minutes
Ingredients:
- Bread Twists Dough
- 120g all-purpose flour
- 1 teaspoon baking powder
- ¼ teaspoon salt
- 150g fat free Greek yogurt
- Brushing
- 2 tablespoons light butter
- 2 tablespoons granulated sugar
- 1-2 teaspoons ground cinnamon, to taste

Directions:
1. Mix flour, salt and baking powder in a bowl.
2. Stir in yogurt and the rest of the dough ingredients in a bowl.
3. Mix well and make 8 inches long strips out of this dough.
4. Twist the strips and place them in the air fryer baskets.
5. Return the air fryer basket 1 to Zone 1, and basket 2 to Zone 2 of the Tefal 2-Basket Air Fryer.
6. Choose the "Air Fry" mode for Zone 1 at 375 degrees F and 15 minutes of cooking time.
7. Select the "MATCH COOK" option to copy the settings for Zone 2.
8. Initiate cooking by pressing the START/PAUSE BUTTON.
9. Flip the twists once cooked halfway through.
10. Mix butter with cinnamon and sugar in a bowl.
11. Brush this mixture over the twists.
12. Serve.

Nutrition:
- (Per serving) Calories 391 | Fat 24g | Sodium 142mg | Carbs 38.5g | Fiber 3.5g | Sugar 21g | Protein 6.6g

Funnel Cake

Servings: 4
Cooking Time: 5 Minutes
Ingredients:
- Coconut, or avocado oil, for spraying
- 110 g self-raising flour, plus more for dusting
- 240 ml fat-free vanilla Greek yogurt
- ½ teaspoon ground cinnamon
- ¼ cup icing sugar

Directions:
1. Preheat the air fryer to 192°C. Line the two air fryer drawers with baking paper, and spray lightly with oil.
2. In a large bowl, mix together the flour, yogurt and cinnamon until the mixture forms a ball.
3. Place the dough on a lightly floured work surface and knead for about 2 minutes.
4. Cut the dough into 4 equal pieces, then cut each of those into 6 pieces. You should have 24 pieces in total.
5. Roll the pieces into 8- to 10-inch-long ropes. Loosely mound the ropes into 4 piles of 6 ropes.
6. Place the dough piles in the two prepared drawers, and spray liberally with oil.
7. Cook for 5 minutes, or until lightly browned.
8. Dust with the icing sugar before serving.

Healthy Semolina Pudding

Servings: 4
Cooking Time: 20 Minutes
Ingredients:
- 45g semolina
- 1 tsp vanilla
- 500ml milk
- 115g caster sugar

Directions:
1. Mix semolina and ½ cup milk in a bowl. Slowly add the remaining milk, sugar, and vanilla and mix well.
2. Pour the mixture into four greased ramekins.
3. Insert a crisper plate in the Tefal air fryer baskets.
4. Place ramekins in both baskets.
5. Select zone 1, then select "air fry" mode and set the temperature to 300 degrees F for 20 minutes. Press "match" to match zone 2 settings to zone 1. Press "start/stop" to begin.

Nutrition:
- (Per serving) Calories 209 | Fat 2.7g | Sodium 58mg | Carbs 41.5g | Fiber 0.6g | Sugar 30.6g | Protein 5.8g

Pumpkin Muffins

Servings:4
Cooking Time:20

Ingredients:
- 1 and ½ cups of all-purpose flour
- ½ teaspoon baking soda
- ½ teaspoon of baking powder
- 1 and 1/4 teaspoons cinnamon, groaned
- 1/4 teaspoon ground nutmeg, grated
- 2 large eggs
- Salt, pinch
- 3/4 cup granulated sugar
- 1/2 cup dark brown sugar
- 1 and 1/2 cups of pumpkin puree
- 1/4 cup coconut milk

Directions:
1. Take 4 ramekins that are the size of a cup and layer them with muffin papers.
2. Crack an egg in a bowl and add brown sugar, baking soda, baking powder, cinnamon, nutmeg, and sugar.
3. Whisk it all very well with an electric hand beater.
4. Now, in a second bowl, mix the flour, and salt.
5. Now, mix the dry ingredients slowly with the wet ingredients.
6. Now, at the end fold in the pumpkin puree and milk, mix it well
7. Divide this batter into 4 ramekins.
8. Now, divide ramekins between both zones.
9. Set the time for zone 1 to 18 minutes at 360 degrees Fat AIRFRY mode.
10. Select the MATCH button for the zone 2 basket.
11. Check if not done, and let it AIR FRY for one more minute.
12. Once it is done, serve.

Nutrition:
- (Per serving) Calories 291| Fat6.4 g| Sodium 241mg | Carbs 57.1g | Fiber 4.4g | Sugar42 g | Protein 5.9g

RECIPES INDEX

A

Air Fried Bacon And Eggs 24
Air Fried Bananas 91
Air Fried Beignets 93
Air Fryer Meatloaves 69
alapeño Poppers And Greek Potato Skins With Olives And Feta 29
Apple Fritters 89
Apple Nutmeg Flautas 88
Apricot-glazed Turkey Tenderloin 61
Asian Chicken 60
Asparagus And Bell Pepper Strata And Greek Bagels 13
Avocado Fries With Sriracha Dip 31

B

Bacon & Spinach Cups 18
Bacon And Egg Omelet 17
Bacon And Spinach Egg Muffins 14
Bacon Cinnamon Rolls 21
Bacon Wrapped Pork Tenderloin 68
Bacon-wrapped Dates Bacon-wrapped Scallops 32
Bacon-wrapped Filet Mignon 80
Bacon-wrapped Shrimp 37
Banana And Raisins Muffins 23
Banana Spring Rolls With Hot Fudge Dip 90
Bang Bang Shrimp With Roasted Bok Choy 41
Bbq Pork Spare Ribs 76
Beef Cheeseburgers 71
Beef Jerky Pineapple Jerky 34
Beef Ribs Ii 75
Beets With Orange Gremolata And Goat's Cheese 83
Bell Pepper Stuffed Chicken Roll-ups 67
Berry Crumble And S'mores 97
Biscuit Balls 16
Blackened Mahimahi With Honey-roasted Carrots 49
Blue Cheese Steak Salad 79
Blueberry Muffins 14
Bo Luc Lac 72
Brazilian Chicken Drumsticks 57
Bread Pudding 96
Breaded Scallops 48
Breakfast Cheese Sandwich 15
Breakfast Frittata 19
Breakfast Pitta 23
Breakfast Potatoes 19
Breakfast Sammies 26
Brown Sugar Garlic Salmon 40
Brussels Sprouts 82
Buffalo Chicken 52
Buffalo Seitan With Crispy Zucchini Noodles 86
Buttermilk Fried Chicken 58
Butter-wine Baked Salmon 45

C

Cajun Catfish Cakes With Cheese 48
Cajun Scallops 50
Cauliflower Avocado Toast And All-in-one Toast 25
Cheddar-ham-corn Muffins 15
Cheesy Baked Eggs 26
Chicken & Broccoli 61
Chicken Kebabs 64
Chicken Legs With Leeks 64
Chicken Shawarma 62

Chicken Strips With Satay Sauce 54
Chicken Thighs With Coriander 52
Chicken Vegetable Skewers 65
Chilean Sea Bass With Olive Relish And Snapper With Tomato 42
Chipotle Drumsticks 54
Chocolate Mug Cakes 92
Cinnamon Air Fryer Apples 26
Cinnamon Apple French Toast 22
Cinnamon Bread Twists 99
Cinnamon Rolls 19
Cinnamon Sugar Dessert Fries 97
Cinnamon-apple Pork Chops 73
Cinnamon-beef Kofta 76
Classic Fish Sticks With Tartar Sauce 47
Coconut Chicken Tenders With Broiled Utica Greens 67
Coconut-custard Pie And Pecan Brownies 91
Cod With Avocado And Garlic Prawns 38
Codfish With Herb Vinaigrette 49
Cornbread 13
Crab Cakes 32
Cracked-pepper Chicken Wings 53
Cream Cheese Shortbread Cookies 97
Crispy Catfish 40
Crispy Plantain Chips 35
Crispy Sesame Chicken 66
Crispy Tortilla Chips 31
Crumbed Chicken Katsu 63
Crustless Peanut Butter Cheesecake And Pumpkin Pudding With Vanilla Wafers 88
Curried Orange Honey Chicken 55

D
Delicious Apple Fritters 89
Double-dipped Mini Cinnamon Biscuits 16

E
Easy Breaded Pork Chops 68
Easy Mini Chocolate Chip Pan Cookie 91
Easy Pancake Doughnuts 18
Egg And Avocado In The Tefal 19
Egg And Bacon Muffins 21

F
Fajita Chicken Strips & Barbecued Chicken With Creamy Coleslaw 62
Fish Sandwich 39
Flavorful Salmon With Green Beans 36
Flavourful Mexican Cauliflower 83
Fresh Mix Veggies In Air Fryer 82
Fried Asparagus 82
Fried Oreos 89
Fried Tilapia 44
Funnel Cake 99

G
Garlic Butter Prawns Scampi & Coconut Prawns 46
Garlic Dill Wings 55
Garlic Herbed Baked Potatoes 87
Garlic Sirloin Steak 78
Garlic-herb Fried Squash 83
Garlic-rosemary Brussels Sprouts 86
Garlic-rosemary Pork Loin With Scalloped Potatoes And Cauliflower 74
General Tso's Chicken 59
Glazed Scallops 51
Gluten-free Spice Cookies 96
Goat Cheese-stuffed Bavette Steak 78
Goat Cheese–stuffed Chicken Breast With Broiled Zucchini And Cherry Tomatoes 66
Green Beans With Baked Potatoes 81
Green Salad With Crispy Fried Goat Cheese And Baked Croutons 85
Grilled Peaches 98

H
Hard Boiled Eggs 20
Healthy Semolina Pudding 99

Herb Lemon Mussels 39
Herb Tuna Patties 39
Honey Banana Oatmeal 14
Honey Glazed Bbq Pork Ribs 70
Honey Pecan Shrimp 48
Honey Teriyaki Tilapia 45
Honey-glazed Chicken Thighs 60

I

Italian Sausage And Cheese Meatballs 80

J

Jalapeño Popper Egg Cups And Cheddar Soufflés 24
Jamaican Fried Chicken 63
Jelly Doughnuts 27
Jerk Tofu With Roasted Cabbage 87
JTater Tots 28
Juicy Paprika Chicken Breast 58

K

Kale And Spinach Chips 82
Kheema Burgers 68
Kielbasa Sausage With Pineapple And Kheema Meatloaf 75

L

Lamb Shank With Mushroom Sauce 78
Lemon Chicken Thighs 56
Lemon Pepper Fish Fillets 47
Lemon-blueberry Muffins 21

M

Maple-pecan Tart With Sea Salt 94
Marinated Chicken Legs 54
Mini Peanut Butter Tarts 92
Miso-glazed Shishito Peppers Charred Lemon Shishito Peppers 33
Mixed Air Fry Veggies 80
Mozzarella Arancini 31
Mozzarella Sticks 34
Mushroom Roll-ups 84

Mustard Rubbed Lamb Chops 72

N

Nigerian Peanut-crusted Bavette Steak 77

O

Orange Chicken With Roasted Snap Peas And Scallions 65
Orange-mustard Glazed Salmon 36

P

Panko-crusted Fish Sticks 37
Peanut Butter, Honey & Banana Toast 98
Pecan Brownies And Cinnamon-sugar Almonds 96
Pecan-crusted Catfish Nuggets With "fried" Okra 44
Pepper Poppers 81
Perfect Parmesan Salmon 35
Pigs In A Blanket With Spinach-artichoke Stuffed Mushrooms 77
Pork Chops With Broccoli 70
Pork Sausage Eggs With Mustard Sauce 20
Potato And Parsnip Latkes With Baked Apples 84
Potatoes Lyonnaise 23
Prawn Dejonghe Skewers 42
Pretzels 30
Puff Pastry 18
Pumpkin Fries 28
Pumpkin Hand Pies Blueberry Hand Pies 95
Pumpkin Muffins 100
Pumpkin-spice Bread Pudding 94

R

Roasted Beef 71
Roasted Garlic Chicken Pizza With Cauliflower "wings" 57

S

S'mores Dip With Cinnamon-sugar Tortillas 93
Salmon Nuggets 40

Salmon Quiche 22
Salmon With Broccoli And Cheese 41
Sausage And Pork Meatballs 79
Sausage Balls With Cheese 35
Sausage Hash And Baked Eggs 27
Sausage Meatballs 73
Sausage-stuffed Peppers 76
Savory Soufflé 24
Savory Sweet Potato Hash 22
Seafood Shrimp Omelet 45
Sesame Bagels 17
Simple Buttery Cod & Salmon On Bed Of Fennel And Carrot 46
Simple Cheesecake 95
Simple Pineapple Sticks And Crispy Pineapple Rings 90
Simply Terrific Turkey Meatballs 56
Smothered Chops 74
Southwestern Fish Fillets 36
Spice-rubbed Chicken Pieces 56
Spicy Fish Fillet With Onion Rings 47
Spicy Lamb Chops 70
Steak Bites With Cowboy Butter 73
Strip Steaks With Hasselback Potatoes 69
Stuffed Bell Peppers 32
Stuffed Mushrooms 29
Sumptuous Pizza Tortilla Rolls 71
Sweet And Spicy Carrots With Chicken Thighs 59
Sweet Potato Hash 17
Sweet Potatoes & Brussels Sprouts 85
Sweet Tilapia Fillets 37
Sweet-and-sour Chicken With Pineapple Cauliflower Rice 53

T

Taco-spiced Chickpeas And Black Bean Corn Dip 33
Tasty Lamb Patties 79
Tasty Parmesan Shrimp 38
Tasty Sweet Potato Wedges 28
Tender Juicy Honey Glazed Salmon 51
Teriyaki Chicken Skewers 60
Thai Chicken Meatballs 55
Thai Prawn Skewers And Lemon-tarragon Fish En Papillote 50
Tilapia With Mojo And Crispy Plantains 43
Tuna Patty Sliders 43
Turkey Burger Patties 52
Turkey Ham Muffins 25
Two-way Salmon 51

W

Walnut Baklava Bites Pistachio Baklava Bites 98
Wholemeal Banana-walnut Bread 15
Wild Rice And Kale Stuffed Chicken Thighs 58
Wings With Corn On The Cob 61

Y

Yummy Chicken Breasts 64

Z

Zucchini With Stuffing 81